A Spiritual Journey of a Young Widow

BREATHE

by

Tanisha A Hall

Cover Design By Diamond Sands
Content Editor Marti Covington
Book Cover Photographer Teresa Hewitt (TH Visual Designs)
Makeup Artist Nzinga Noel
Book Design by Custom Made For You

ISBN 978-0999440407

PREFACE

The Path from Love to Loss to Renewed Life

At age 15, I met the man I wanted to marry. I fulfilled my dreams with him nine years later. Then, six months later he suffered a brain aneurysm in the middle of the night. That unexpected illness claimed his life. We were both twenty-four, and I was completely unprepared to lose him, be alone and suffer the ravages of grief.

When I look back, I understand there was a lot I didn't know. I never knew that I would be in love at a young age. I had no idea that one casual conversation in a school hallway would lead to marriage. I never knew I would have a storybook romance. But once love came into my life, I was confident it wouldn't end until I was a very old woman.

My husband's name was Jermaine. He was charming, funny, and athletic. I met him at the end of my freshman year in high school. He changed my perspective on life. But he did that for a lot of people. I can't say he was perfect. No one is. However, just about everyone who knew him would tell you he had a lot of positive attributes. He also had a healthy approach to life. He even had a healthy diet and tried to keep me from eating junk food. Those practices are some of the many reasons why it just seems impossible that he's gone.

Jermaine and I were connected since tenth grade, when we had our first class together. By the middle of the semester that year, something had changed between us. Soon we were talking and texting all the time. By the middle of our sophomore year, we made it official.

Now I know there are thousands of people who have important high school romances. But no one can ever convince me that any other couple had the connection Jermaine and I shared because we were deeply in love.

That doesn't mean we didn't have the typical high school dating experience. We broke up, got back together and repeated the cycle. Even when moments were not the greatest, we chose to stay together and during the next nine years, our relationship blossomed.

At this point I want to address thoughts some of you may have. I know my love for Jermaine may not seem serious because my 'years' of love happened before age 30. That means some people don't see it as an adult relationship, but they should. Losing my husband of six months and boyfriend of nine years was just as deeply devastating to me as to someone who found love later in life at a more 'appropriate' age.

Jermaine was a very likeable guy. He was also a very caring individual and considerate to everyone, no matter a person's shortcomings. Jermaine always wanted to help people. That's probably the reason he became a firefighter. It also reinforces why no one expected him to pass away young. Firefighters have to be fit. They take physicals. There was no way for me to know that I would be a widow at age 24. There was also no way for me to understand that something as simple as a headache was the only clue either of us would have about the severity of an illness that would cause him to slip from this life into the next.

I also didn't know that his transition would totally destroy my life and expectations of living, because I was 'overcome by grief.' That phrase is commonplace. But it's real. It's like drowning when you don't know how to swim. I don't know about this personally, but grief, at the level I experienced it, might be compared to the way drugs can rule a person's life. Grief ruled me like that.

This is a book about grief, and closely tied to it is regret. I blamed myself for not making my husband go to the doctor. I knew he had headaches; I just didn't know their severity. Even the morning he woke up, I asked him if he wanted to go to the doctor and he said no. It's been three years since that morning, and I no longer tear myself to pieces about not forcing him to seek medical care. But you have to know that I've replayed the scenario several thousand times. I have even dreamed of how different my life would be if he would have gone to the doctor earlier. But the hard facts are that we didn't make that decision and he's not here. After all the self- recrimination, I realized I had to change my mindset. So now I try to remember how good we were together instead of focusing on my loss.

The reason I'm sharing all of this information with you is to help you understand the mental, physical, and spiritual connection Jermaine and I shared. Now that he's gone, dates on the calendar that I expected to celebrate for the rest of my life have become confusing for me. For example, every year that Jermaine's birthday comes and goes, I don't know how to act. It reminds me that I miss my best friend. I miss seeing him and just giving him random kisses and hugs. I miss the opportunity of letting him know how much I truly care. Cared.

I want this book to encourage all couples in love to cherish each other. Love your mate beyond your ups and downs. Be there for your loved ones no matter what. I will forever remember the moments we shared together. I love that he loved me in spite of my faults. So, on Jermaine's birthday I sit in house we once shared together and tell him happy birthday – sometimes in tears.
If I could go back, I would really let him know how much I appreciated him. I knew we

would have a life together but did not expect it to end so soon. My marriage to Jermaine was one of the most wonderful moments in my life. We had a home, were in one accord, and had started working on a family. Everything was going perfectly. The plan that I had always envisioned for my life was all coming together. However, six months later I learned to see a different side of love and relationships.

I learned to cherish every person in my life. I learned to embrace the individuals who embraced me. I also learned that anything can be taken without cause or reason. Any and everything can change, leaving nothing but memories. I learned to expect the unexpected. I had never lived my life like that, and I absolutely hated it. The unexpected aspects, self- récrimination and grief overwhelmed me. I wrote this book to keep myself sane.

Grief has turned me into a different person. I also wrote this book to share my walk away from the pain of losing my husband. It's been a hard journey. If you really want to know who you are, analyze what comes out of your mouth. Words reflect what's really going on in your heart. I never knew how ambitious and positive I was until I read what I had written two years ago in my journal.
My fight with grief has taught me that life is never full of roses. Sometimes it will give you weeds and flowers growing together. Your job is to separate the beauty from the trash to create your own unique and beautiful garden. If you, like me, are young and have lost someone you love, I want you to read the words I've written and help find your own purpose. This book is about grief, but it was composed to uplift, inspire, encourage, and challenge readers.

Life is never going to be good all the time. What it can be however, is a lesson of hope, of inspiration, even when life throws rocks at you.

Before I lost my husband, I thought that I could handle anything. Then, I had one major setback in my life, and it challenged both my faith and self-image. I still haven't mastered the meaning of life; perhaps I never will. But I do know it's simultaneously full of purpose while also beautiful and a vapor. Love who you are, laugh at the crazy and wonderful moments in your life, and live to start another day. You'll never know what it will bring. My experience has made me realize that we have one moment and time to be happy, and the very next instant, something unexpected may happen.

Becoming a widow was unexpected and unwanted. But three years after the fact, I am at a point where I am able to enjoy life again. Getting here was a process. It would have been easier if someone had told me what to expect. That's why I wrote this book.

It is my sincere hope that you join me while I share my self-reflections complied over the last two years. I want my words to help you focus on your own personal growth, even when loss seems to dominate all of your thoughts. You are stronger than you think, and life can be good even when the love of your life has passed on.

INTRODUCTION

Grief is like a roller-coaster. One minute you think that you have mastered it, and the next it reminds you that you are still on the ride. Be ready for the ride of anger, disappointment, and disbelief. In addition, you also have the pit stop of jealously that seems to never end, because you are always comparing your life to those of other people. I have found myself wondering what was so wrong with me that my life had to be damaged beyond anything I was able to understand.

The roller-coaster of grief tosses you from side to side, and you never know when it's going to end. When grief gripped me, I would look at other people and wonder if my life could be good ever again. Full-blown grief escalates disappointment into depression. The introspective nature of grief also provides lots of opportunities for emotional self-abuse. The feeling of anger, for me, became so uncontrollable that it seemed like I'd lost the ability to stay sane. There was no safe haven. Everything felt like a threat. I am a person of faith and tried reaching toward God in the hope that He could take me away from the nightmarish path my life had taken.

I wanted off the roller-coaster ride of grief. It had shaken me up so much that I no longer recognized myself. Grief stole my ability to believe that everything was going be all right. I knew life was a journey, but this was not the way I wanted to continue traveling on it.

In the beginning, I turned to sources of strength that had worked in my life before. My mind turned toward Bible scriptures that promised me that I would "stand against all the fiery darts of the evil one." But at one point, my problem was the darts that seemed to originate in my heart. My inner struggle and the inability to move forward caused me the most torment. Grief made me question everything. I didn't recognize anything about myself or my actions. Yes, I also questioned God. I'm supposed to believe this was the life that God had given me? If that's true, why does it feel so horrible? Why do I feel like this pain is afflicting every aspect of my life?

All grief, all the time just breaks you down. I was tired and ready for something better, something great. Even more, I was ready to get off the grief roller-coaster because nothing I had ever done prepared me for this whiplash ride. I wanted to be normal. I just didn't know what that was.

What I can tell you, after losing my husband in 2014, is that the normal I wanted or expected before his death was never going to be my reality. I had to understand several new facts about my life. The first thing I had to learn was that I was not the same person. I wasn't a bride. I wasn't a wife. I was a widow. Let's correct that. I was a young widow, and I absolutely hated it. I hated the comforting words from strangers who had heard about 'my loss.' I hated how friends treated me. I hated my job. I hated other newlyweds. It upset me to see mothers with new babies. But beyond getting easily upset was the anger. There were many times I was angry with my family. There were other times that hate and anger combined to make me despise myself and be angry with the God who made me.

Those feelings dominated me for about a month. The next five months didn't feel much better, but I did take steps to rebuild my life. I sought help, several times. I prayed. I tried to socialize. I changed careers. Some things worked. Some were a disaster. But what I found was a new person. That new person was me. There was still pain. There was still a lot of confusion. I still wasn't healed and was trying to get off the grief roller-coaster. However, it had slowed down enough to let me try.

One year after I lost my husband, I redeveloped the ability to examine my feelings. I also started to manage my expectations of other people more rationally. I began to see my own mistakes. I also saw that no one really knew how to interact with me. It took me a year to see that most were trying to do the best they knew how to do.

Two years after my husband's death, I was off the grief roller-coaster. But looking back, I know that it would have happened sooner if someone had told me things I had to figure out myself. I wasn't crazy. It's okay to be angry, and yes, all of those horrible feelings did pass. I am getting my life back. But it's not the life I had dreamed about living. What I expected from my life was predictable. Now my life is more of an adventure and one I'm willing to share in the pages of this book.

This book doesn't offer advice. It simply shows the path I followed that allowed me to come to grips with grief. It's organized by topics that affect every grieving widow or widower younger than thirty. But within each topic is something I call a 'grief timeline.' The first two weeks after my loss, I was shocked and emotionally numb. But by the first

Tanisha A. Hall

thirty days, it's a different story. You'll find out what I mean when you read this book. Right at six months, I had an entirely different set of feelings and experiences. At one year, I realized I had become a different person, but not necessarily one I liked. By year two, I was off the grief roller-coaster ride and on my way to building a new life. In three sections of this book, I've asked two professionals (a family friend and medical physician Tuere Coulter, M.D. and a clinical psychologist and professional counselor, Shaneka McClarty L.P.C., N.C.C.) to describe the physical ways grief affected me and or explain why certain sights, sounds, or places would cause a flood of emotion. This book will also address my conflicts with faith and conclude by letting you read what I have learned as a young widow.

My goal is to show you why healing from grief takes time and why the experiences of a young person who has lost a mate are vastly different from those of any other age group. I hope this book helps the families of young people who are grieving because the person they have loved has transitioned. I hope this book helps friends, and above all I hope it explains the grieving process in a way that's relevant to the people who read it.

Grief is hard. But it can be conquered. Please look at my life and see some of the ways that can be done.

Tanisha A. Hall

SELF-PERCEPTION

1

*Grief forced me to live for myself
and not as someone's wife or daughter.*

Tanisha A. Hall

SELF-PERCEPTION
@30 DAYS

Until my husband was buried, I had never lived life for myself. From birth until our wedding day, I was somebody's daughter. Then I became a wife – which I thought was wonderful.

Since tenth grade I'd had one goal. I wanted to marry a boy I met in ninth grade and bear his children. I wanted to become his Mrs. That was my identity. It was who I aspired to be. It was all I wanted to become. Now, that doesn't mean I was living my life on hold. I graduated from college with great grades, had friends, and loved interacting with my family. But my focus was on being a wife and mother as soon as possible.

When my wedding took place, I felt I had achieved one of my most important ambitions. I was unbelievably happy and I remained so until the day my husband woke up with a headache, went to the hospital, and passed away.

What I didn't realize in that hospital room was that his transition also marked one of my own. It started with my new definition in society. I wasn't someone's wife. I couldn't go back to being my parents' daughter. I was a widow. I had no idea what that meant and even worse, I had no idea how people would treat me because of my changed status. I really didn't know anything. I just knew that I hurt. The hurt, combined with my grief, made the change I had to make even more traumatic. I was becoming a person consumed with pain and hopelessness. I didn't understand that then. But what I wish is that someone had told me about what was going to happen.

Tanisha A. Hall

SELF-PERCEPTION

2

I tried to 'socialize' based on someone else's timetable, but I wasn't ready.

Tanisha A. Hall

SELF-PERCEPTION
@SIX MONTHS

Six months had passed since I buried my husband, Jermaine. Coming to terms with being single was almost as painful as losing the only man I ever loved, my husband, Jermaine. I thought I was taking steps that would help me move on in my life when I attended a singles outreach at church. The group had scheduled a lunch get-together after the service. I could handle that, right? Wrong. I was still heart-broken. The depth of my hurt displayed itself before church ended. I had to fight tears welling up in my eyes, and then I began to shake. I got in my car and literally cried all the way to the restaurant.

Technically, I knew I was starting over in life. But what I couldn't understand was why I could only see the negative side-effects of this new person I had to become. Could somebody please help me understand why on earth did I not want to accept the fact that I truly was SINGLE?

Truth be told, I would have rather been called a widow than a single lady. Hearing that phrase really made me cringe! Yes, I was single, but I also was not ready to accept it. I was not ready to live in the new reality everybody else seemed to accept for me so easily. I just wasn't ready to do it. But what was wrong with that? I mean, wasn't it okay for me to be true to myself and not pretend like I was happy to be single? Why did my feelings have to match other people's expectations?

That's where the confusion started. There is no one right answer. Of course, there were several ways to look at everything. I chose to focus on being truthful to myself. But truth came with consequences. For me, that meant lying in bed a lot of days and nights, with a real case of the blues. My life was not where I wanted it to be, and that kept me in a state of perpetual sadness. There was still a lot of pain and disappointment inside of me. When I thought about it, there were several reasons why. I can list them easily now in 2017. Six months after my husband died, I couldn't.

But it was really simple. I really wasn't ready to move on emotionally. I was not ready to date, and most of all, I was NOT ready for love.

Love to me then meant going through the back-and-forth of learning someone else's feelings. That's a lot of work I saw no reason to do. Additionally, I was on the fence about joining the singles ministry or even attending another event. However, the singles ministry event did serve a positive purpose. I learned something. What I did find out that day was that I needed more time. It was going to take more than six months for me to sort through my feelings and more time than that to heal. I didn't know how long it would take to face my single-ism, (if that is a word.) I was still a work in progress. Hey, one little milestone was better than none. Writing about the singles luncheon helped me sort what I was really feeling from what everyone was telling me I ought to feel.

Maybe someday I will meet someone new and be more open to a romantic friendship. But that's going to happen when I am fully ready. In the meantime, my reality is that no matter what, I still love my hubby and never want to forget him.

The singles ministry day was not the best for me. However, I overcame something. I overcame being alone and accepted being single for a full ninety minutes. That's a step in the right direction.

SELF-PERCEPTION

3

*I am now aware that other people
hurt and no one gets
to magically beat the odds.*

Tanisha A. Hall

SELF-PERCEPTION
@ONE YEAR

I am more aware every day that I'm not the only person who has had their life changed by some type of terrible pain. People are hurting in plain sight everywhere. I was getting my nails done when I happened to see a lady who seemed as if she had gone through some sort of illness. I wanted to have a conversation with her but didn't. I didn't want to come off as insensitive.

However, I have started to realize that we all have some type of pain that has left a wound. Some of those wounds show physically; for example, the lady who lost all of her hair due to chemotherapy. Her hair loss is a scar that reminds her of pain. For me, the source of my pain was losing my husband. I will never have the chance to see him again in this life. The thought of him makes me hurt and ask myself, "Do I deserve such pain? Do I deserve to be left in the dark in regards to my future?"

Not knowing how my future will unfold is really scary. The unfortunate truth is: that's life. No one deserves to just magically beat the odds and win a clean sweep in the lottery of life. However, that's not what I grew up believing. As a young girl, I always felt like I deserved good things in life. Now, I know that no one deserves anything. The lady I noticed at the nail salon does not deserve sickness. The lady who just lost her son overseas does not deserve to bury her child. I am learning that things happen in this world, whether a person is good or bad. We, as a people, are not always going to experience an existence of beauty with no pain.

When my husband's headache sent him to the hospital and put him in in coma, I refused to accept the likely outcome of his diagnosis. I didn't think I deserved to be a widow. Yet, Jermaine did not survive, and I had to ask myself hard questions. Some of them I still can't answer.

What I do know is that life can bring us to moments where we need to stretch and grow. There's a quote from Bernice Johnson Reagon, a civil rights activist who founded the acapella group Sweet Honey in the Rock, that soothes me when I think about how unfair everything can be. She wrote, "Life's challenges are not supposed to paralyze you; they're supposed to help you discover who you are."

Ms. Reagon's observation really brought things that have happened to me into perspective, because I really am finding out who this person called me - is. I am truly finding out the what, how, and where of ME. I have never had to do that before. I am expanding and growing beyond my wildest imagination. I am finding myself doing things that I would have never imagined myself doing this time last year. Sometimes, it is good to be expanded and stretched beyond the limitations of our own thoughts.

I now know I am a strong and tough cookie. I am also really beginning to see the light out of my horrific storm of grief. Every new shift in movement creates a change in response. My hope for my life is to grow and find meaning in every storm or season I face. I also hope that those who read my journals and this book find reasons of their own to stretch beyond measure and become better than ever. None of us should come out of the storms that blow past us as bitter individuals. We should be joyful for the experience that has changed our attitude and lives.

It's only when we stay encouraged and embrace the change that we can be set free.

Tanisha A. Hall

SELF-PERCEPTION

4

I have to focus on the present and not the past.

Tanisha A. Hall

SELF-PERCEPTION
@TWO YEARS

Somehow, and in some way, I got lost. I got so caught up in the hype of love and marriage that I forgot all about keeping myself in check. "I am looking for something that I cannot obtain," is what I constantly tell myself. I was looking for love in all the wrong places.

I spent a lot of time thinking about how my life started to spiral out of control because of my past pain. Why my life? What had I done so wrong to deserve this? It felt as if I was constantly blaming God and loved the joy of being in misery.

I'd been selfish, and I didn't realize it. I loved the comfort that I received from people, yet had neglected the people who I needed to help me move on. What have I done with my life in the past two years, I ask myself. Why have I allowed one tragedy in my life to determine my story? One problem was I've tried to stop feeling.

I mask my feelings in sorrow. I mask my feelings in insecurity. My self-esteem drops, and then I make decisions based on nonsense. That's weird, and I know it now. But at the time I had no idea about what I had become. I became a lost soul searching for things that gave me no true pleasure in life. Instead of trying to find happiness, I dug myself more deeply into worldly possessions hoping that what I looked for would come to me. I wanted to be happy.

Yet I knew I couldn't find happiness by buying the latest bags, keeping my hair and nails done. Each day, I woke up hoping to find special love again. However, my heart wouldn't let me. Then the grief-filled bitterness would set in. My mind would go back to what God didn't do and how He did not come through. Yet the small still voice inside of me would say, "Tanisha, let go. Let go, you cannot fight this on your own."

My emotions went up and down. My mind spun constantly, and the only person who could truly solve the problem was me.

I made myself crazy trying to figure everything out. I had to stop trying to search for answers that might not come. However, it was hard being able to accept the things that I couldn't change and be positive about the things in life yet to come. Then I reached the conclusion that I could put away some of the pain if I stopped expecting everything to go my way. I had to learn how to breathe and let the pain, worry, and cares of this life go.

My first step was to acknowledge where I was in life. The next step, for me, was to truly have a heart that was spiritually motivated. The final step I had to take was the hardest. But it was where the healing really started. I had to stop complaining and also stop focusing on things that didn't make sense to me.
I had to start focusing on the present and not the past. When I continued to think about complaints, that became my focus. The key to the healing, for me, was to recognize that I tried to do it in my own power. That was not possible, and I was determined to go back to the One who has carried every burden that I try to keep.

As I look back and reflect on the attitudes, beliefs, and thoughts two years after my husband died, I have realized that I wasn't the same person who I used to be before April 12. Now don't get me wrong, I still have moments of uncertainty, but it surely is not as bad as it used to be. I used to be so doubtful in my faith and hope in God. I have come to understand that I am getting stronger each day. I used to think that I wasn't strong. I couldn't see my strength. I'm still here, in my right mind, so I must be some type of strong! I have gained strength and peace in some type of way via Jesus. I am also beginning to look at life, friendships, and the characters of others differently.

My mother said something very important to me at this time. She said, "Celebrate with people who celebrate you!" For the longest time, I did things because I knew my husband would want it. But now, my husband is no longer here. So, I started doing what was best for me and not best for my husband. It took a minute for me to get to that point. My husband's stepmom said it in the best way. She said, "You need to live for you and find who you are."
I truly believe that this became a season for me to find who in the world Tanisha was. I have lived through Jermaine and me. I lived through maintaining our relationship. As much as it hurts to not see Jermaine, it was important for me to move beyond the hurt. I may have had moments of sadness, but I wouldn't let sadness be the start of my new life. I take this opportunity as a way to build my faith in God, do things that I enjoy, and not make irrational decisions. As bad as it may seem, I have made irrational decisions

that I never thought twice about. But, I'm now in a place where I won't make a final decision based on temporary emotions. That's a truth that I can honestly say I am still working on.

In regards to friendships, I'm learning that everyone is not going to love me. Everyone is not going to be there for you. Everyone is not going to celebrate my success. Also, people who were for you may not be with you for a lifetime. There are seasons in life and even in friendships.

As I mentioned before, I did things just because of what I thought Jermaine would think and want. But, the season of me and Jermaine has ended. I have to keep pushing for me and be guided through Christ. Therefore, I have decided that I am going to start living. I will not waste energy on foolishness, drama, and hurt. I cannot afford to deal with those things if I expect greatness. I'm living, taking back my peace and joy. I am going to celebrate with others about marriage and even childbirth. Though it hurts that I am not a mother as planned, I'm going to be happy for other mothers whom I know. As I end this chapter in my life, I open the book to a new chapter that is titled 'Start Living'; living beyond hurt. I'm going to live to fulfill my purpose. Therefore, I choose to be happy, and I will be happy. Happiness is within reach; we just have to take the necessary steps.

Tanisha A. Hall

GRIEF-BASED
MENTAL AND PHYSICAL PAIN

1

Grief gripped me physically and began to affect
my ability to function rationally.

Tanisha A. Hall

GRIEF-BASED MENTAL AND PHYSICAL PAIN @30 DAYS

A few hours after the doctors told us that Jermaine was, in fact, brain dead I was at a complete loss about how I was supposed to live my life. I wanted so badly to go back to the house and start over. I remember walking into our room re-living the events from the day before. It was as if nothing changed and everything was the same, except I knew Jermaine was never coming home.

I couldn't stand it. So, a day later, I moved back into my parent's home. I couldn't take another minute being in the home where Jermaine and I used to live. It was too hard waking up in that house and having it be a constant reminder of my new reality. All day, every day, the first person on my mind was Jermaine and the last person on my mind was Jermaine. All I could do was eat, sleep, and breath Jermaine. I could not get him out of my mind. Strange questions confronted me day and night. I wanted to know if Jermaine was okay and how he could have passed so suddenly at such a young age.

For the first few weeks, I wondered if he were in pain or if he were in heaven or hell. I was hard on myself during this time, because I wanted so badly to believe that his death wasn't my fault.

On top of feeling sorry for myself, my grief made me sick. I had anxiety attacks. I am not sure when the headaches and chest pains started; all I know was that they increased to the point that they really worried me. I started to wonder when death was going to knock on my door.

Thoughts of death or dying never crossed my mind until the doctors had confirmed that Jermaine's brain had stopped working. It was hard to think that someone you just had a conversation with over the phone had transitioned. All I knew was that my headaches and chest pain and the flashbacks of seeing Jermaine passing out on the floor from a seizure were wearing me down mentally and physically. I struggled with my flashbacks. I tried my hardest to not think about the early morning tragedy that claimed my husband's life, but I couldn't make the movie inside my head stop.

My body and mind played tricks on me. I can remember several times thinking I was about to pass out because my anxiety was so high. There was one time at 3 a.m. that my heart and mind raced so hard that it woke me up. It felt as if I were reliving the moments when I saw Jermaine pass out on the floor. Death seemed to stalk me because I constantly thought about how easily it could change your life without warning. My chest began to hurt, and the feeling of my heart pounding terrified me. I could feel my breath slowly going away.

Then my ability to focus began to slip. My surroundings were beginning to slowly look unfamiliar. I started to be afraid that I was going to fall out and never again see the reality of life again. However, what was really happening was I had started to give in to grief and lose control over my life and thoughts. I responded by staying in bed. I started having full-blown conversations in my head that no one knew about. It was a struggle to know the difference between the 'here and now' and mere thoughts.

When I tried to explain what was happening to me, people told me to control it. But how do you control something that you have never experienced before? How can you capture something that has no form? What does it take to manage thoughts that are spiraling out of control?

I was trying so hard to balance everything, but it was just impossible. Since I couldn't be happy on my own, I tried to pretend. But I became a nervous wreck because thoughts about death consumed me. I was afraid because I did not want to die, and yet the thoughts and physical pain I experienced confirmed that death could happen to anyone without notice. It was as if all I could anticipate were bad things. I kept my guard up so death would not catch me by surprise, the way it caught my 24-year-old husband.

What I didn't understand at the time is that I had set a pattern for myself that could never help me heal. The phrase 'overcome by grief' never occurred to me. It just happened.

Tanisha A. Hall

Tuere Coulter, MD; Family Medicine
A Doctor's Statement about Grief

Grief can affect us emotionally, physically, and socially. Symptoms of grief can be sadness, anger, guilt, anxiety, crying, loss of appetite, irregular sleep patterns, social withdrawal, depression, and post-traumatic stress disorder. People experiencing grief may also develop headaches, weakness, fatigue, aches and pains in muscles and joints, a feeling of heaviness, or an uneasy feeling in the pit of their stomach. When grieving, a person can have only one or a combination of the symptoms stated. Although grief is a natural process, it can become complicated, which means it can become prolonged and even disabling.

Tanisha A. Hall

GRIEF-BASED
MENTAL AND PHYSICAL PAIN

2

If there is such a thing as GTSD –
Grief Traumatic Stress Disorder – I had it.

MENTAL AND PHYSICAL PAIN
@SIX MONTHS

Six months after we buried my husband, I felt like I was living in a dream. It was a bad one based on some pretend world that I never wanted to visit. It felt like I was here and not here. Grief gripped everything about me and made me feel like I was having an out-of-body experience. The world I used to live in no longer looked familiar to me.

I was sick but not necessarily ill. I knew something was wrong but never could understand what. I Googled my symptoms. I tried to find someone who had experienced the same thing as I had. The only results that I could get suggested that I potentially had a detachment disorder, PTSD, or was clinically depressed. Duh. I had started taking classes for an advanced degree. One of the topics discussed was Post Traumatic Stress Disorder. My symptoms didn't jive with what the educator described. Yet I still had flashbacks. Maybe there's such a thing as GTSD. Grief Traumatic Stress Disorder. If so, I definitely had it.

My main goal at this time was to find someone else who felt the way I did. I wanted to talk to other widows who had faced something similar. I believed that if I could find someone else who felt the way I did, then it meant I wasn't crazy. But the problem was I didn't know anyone like me. Every other widow I knew was at least in her thirties and had spent years with a spouse. No widow I knew was young. No one truly understood my debilitating anguish.

The chest pains still continued, but now they were bad enough to put me in the emergency room. My blood pressure was high, which contributed to my physical anxiety. In addition to the anger and pain, I was also afraid. I was always dizzy and didn't know why. But when I went to the doctor, I learned that my blood pressure was roughly 140/90. I was so shocked. I mean, I knew that I was having panic attacks, but I just didn't know the effects. The doctor checked me three times: once sitting up, another lying down, and another standing up. All in all, my lowest blood pressure was when I was lying down. That would explain why I felt comfortable and safe in bed. The pain that I experienced after losing Jermaine was unimaginable. It was like someone sticking a knife through me, and here I was hoping to heal from the wound without getting any medical help.

My spiritual health was low, too. I was angry with God. Let me be blunt, I was over God. I did not want to pray to a God who obviously didn't listen and who ignored me. I even shared those feelings with my mother. I felt alone – I felt as if the God that I grew up worshipping was not the same God unable to come through for me.

I grew up believing that you had no right to be angry with God. But after Jermaine was buried, I would tell people who chided me for my anger that "He knows everything, so He knows if you're mad anyway." So why deprive yourself a feeling that He already knows you have? I decided when Jermaine passed that I was not going to be passive with my feelings towards God. I was not going to pretend that I worshipped God at church when I felt that He could have stopped everything that transpired. Beyond my anger was emotional pain. I was hurt every time I looked at married couples, engaged couples, and mothers who had kids.

It got to the point that I hated going out in public. Whenever I came back from an event or function, I would rush straight to bed and watch my paid-TV service. Being in bed was a safe place for me. Part of it was my physical self wanted to lie down all of the time because that was the only time I didn't feel dizzy. The loss, the constant thoughts of the day my husband of six months passed out, and my inability to completely understand what was real and what wasn't made my pain unbearable. The worst part was no one seemed to understand my torment, which means no one knew how to help.

Tanisha A. Hall

Tuere Coulter, MD; Family Medicine
A Doctor's Statement about Grief

If grief begins to become disruptive in your life, such as affecting personal relationships, family dynamics, or your day-to-day activities, I encourage you to schedule your appointment and speak with your physician. There are treatment options including counseling and medication as well.

Tanisha A. Hall

GRIEF-BASED
MENTAL AND PHYSICAL PAIN

3

It took a full twelve months for me to internally understand that my husband was never coming back.

Tanisha A. Hall

MENTAL AND PHYSICAL PAIN
@ONE YEAR

It took a year, but my headaches finally stopped. However, I still had chest pains, and my life still felt like it was some sort of dream. It was still hard to leave the house because I was always dizzy. I always felt like I was going to pass out at any given moment. It was as if someone had spun me around several times, and I was trying to regain my focus. But it had happened long enough for me to know it was the effects of grief.

The first year of grief makes you feel as if you are going crazy. I lived in my head most of the time. I continually wondered if I were truly having a psychotic breakdown. I kept seeking answers and alternately felt like I was schizophrenic, clinically depressed, bi-polar, or any of several other varieties of mental disease that exist. The more I read, the longer the list was. I kept trying to find ways to help myself because I couldn't find anyone who could help me.

I still had flashbacks from the night my husband fell out on the floor of our home. That memory really left me twisted. Whenever I saw someone "look" as if they were going to pass out, I would burst into tears. I remember one day I was in a seafood restaurant, and a customer slipped and fell. The woman hurt herself, but in the world inside my mind, I thought she was going to die. I wanted so badly to run out of there. I started crying because it felt like it was the night my husband, Jermaine had his seizure, all over again. But it didn't take a fall to freak me out. Someone just had to cough wrong, and I had a quick flashback to the trauma that I experienced with my late 24-year-old husband.

The first twelve months after my husband passed was a really hard time for me. The physical pain was lessening, and yet my anxiety was still there. I was constantly thinking about thinking and trying to figure out if there was truly something wrong with me. I didn't want to be alone and relied on my parents like a child. I even ended up joining a church because it was close to my parents' home. Whenever I had to leave the house, I would always call my best friend to go with me. She was my go-to person, the one who helped me figure things out.

I'm writing this three years after Jermaine transitioned. But the truth is that first year really felt like a blur. There's a lot I don't remember. My new life did not feel or seem real. I felt detached from the world and everyone around me. At the same time, I was very forgetful, emotional, and angry. If I could sum up the first year, I would say it was when reality set in. I was going to live my life without Jermaine, and nothing was going to change that. There was nothing I could do about it. It took me a year to accept that. Everything was totally different, and now I had to start building a new reality – a reality that I never wanted to live, much less understand.

Tuere Coulter, MD; Family Medicine
A Doctor's Statement about Grief

Family and friends should be supportive during the grieving process. There may be times where those grieving may appear to not be interested in communicating with you. They may become withdrawn, but this is not a personal attack against the friend or family member, but a part of their grieving process. Continue to reach out to them...and encourage them to seek help if their symptoms become concerning.

Tanisha A. Hall

GRIEF-BASED
MENTAL AND PHYSICAL PAIN

4

*After two years, I embraced the good
in my life that came from grief.*

Tanisha A. Hall

MENTAL AND PHYSICAL PAIN
@TWO YEARS

More than two years have gone by since my husband passed away at age 24. I no longer lie in my bed binge-watching paid programming because I am too tired and/or sad to leave my room. I can finally eat food without worrying about my blood pressure, and I've stopped being afraid to sleep in an empty house by myself. I've made progress in other areas, as well. I am no longer worried about which direction my life will take now that I am living it without Jermaine. Yes, there are times when I think about him, but now there are also times where I think about the happy moments we shared. The emotional breakdowns have stopped. I do miss Jermaine and wish that he were here with me. I also wish that I were still married to him. But now I know that I have to finally close this chapter in my life. I finally have to let go of grief.

I know that I can't keep holding on to a memory when I also want it to end. I have finally allowed myself to realize that life does go on whether we want it to or not. There are going to be times where you just lose control and other times where you still feel stuck. Grief has been and will always be a roller-coaster ride where you have really low lows and really high highs. There's a reason why the phrase 'overcome by grief' exists.

However, the beautiful thing about grief is that you get to reinvent yourself. You get an opportunity to work on things that you may have never considered. You get to accomplish that dream that you always envisioned. And believe it or not, you get an opportunity to find new hobbies that you may have never had the chance to try.

The physical and mental pain does fade. There are times where those old debilitating thoughts creep into my head. Now I can put them in line. I also don't hide from being around people. In fact, it's gotten easier for me to effectively deal with my loss and my anxiety. I am in no way saying that things are always easy yet. I am saying that I have started to move forward and now know that life can be what you decide to make it.

Things happen in life that are beyond our control. Our job is to learn that everything is and will always be okay; we just may not see that clearly at the time.

MEMORIES

1

*The day my husband passed and the day
we buried him will always scar my
heart but not destroy my life.*

Tanisha A. Hall

MEMORIES
@30 DAYS

There are two days that will forever send a pang of pain through my heart. They are the day my husband passed and the day he was buried.

Everything that happened the day my husband left this life has stayed fresh in my memory, whether I have wanted it to or not. It started with a panic attack that gripped me while I rode with my parents back from visit to a college several hours away.

I was so scared. It felt as if I were having some sort of chest pain or heart attack. It was a physical manifestation of grief and one I would experience many times over the next two years.

My apprehension had actually started earlier in the day. Something didn't feel right to me – even before my parents dropped me off at the home Jermaine and I shared. My family and I had taken a day-long road trip. My husband Jermaine was supposed to go but stayed home because he had a training session for the fire department.

I went into the room where Jermaine was sleeping and decided to get some rest myself before going to work in the morning. That didn't happen. I spent the night wrestling with this sick feeling that something was wrong. I just couldn't put my finger on what it was. Since I was restless, I slept in the guest bedroom so my husband would have a better night's sleep. I knew that he was suffering from a headache and wanted him to be comfortable in bed. However, I felt compelled to go back in the room with him. When I got there, I took a shower to feel better but actually became more nervous.

I told my husband I couldn't sleep, and he told me to calm down. I said a prayer and drifted off.

But at 3:00 a.m. Jermaine shot up out of bed and told me his head hurt. I asked him if he wanted to go to the emergency room. He responded no. But his speech was slurred. I thought to myself, "What is he talking about?" Then he collapsed, and that was the last conversation that I had with him.

At first, I didn't understand what I was seeing. I thought he fell down as a joke. Then he started moaning. I realized that he hit the floor pretty hard, and he was not answering my questions. I jumped out of the bed and turned the lights on. That's when I saw he was having a seizure. I was in complete shock and was hysterical when I called 911. I told the dispatcher what I thought I was seeing, which turned out to be true. He indeed had a seizure, which in turn was the cause of his aneurysm.

My memories after that are a series of blurs. I only had one thought. I wanted to believe that Jermaine was going to make it. I even sent him a text stating that once this was all over we were going to look back and laugh. Yet signs weren't looking good. He had stopped breathing for a short time at home, and when he was brought back to consciousness his breathing wasn't normal.

At the hospital, I wanted to believe that God would raise him up like Lazarus. If ever there was a time that I needed God, this was it. I needed God to help Jermaine come back better than ever. As my husband lay in the hospital bed, I whispered in his ear that I loved him and that we had to have kids together.
However, the doctors burst my positive prayer bubble a few minutes later when they told me that Jermaine didn't make it. He was deceased.

My whole life shattered at 3:40 that morning. It was no longer Jermaine and me against the world. Suddenly, it was just me trying to figure out what had just happened. I could not for the life of me understand how you can go from having it all to watching every hope you had slip away.

But there was another huge heartache to come, the funeral. For the person who has suffered a loss like this, there are two stages of pain-numbing sadness. You have to plan the funeral, and then you have to attend it. Who thinks about burying their husband at age 24? I didn't. The whole process gave me panic attacks. What it didn't do was give me a chance to grieve or cry. We're told that funerals are for the living to mourn. That's not really true when you're only 24 and burying your husband of six months. Part of me just checked out and for that reason there were moments it felt like Jermaine had gone on an extended stay away from me. Yet I knew that wasn't true.

Again, I was blessed because I had support that made the entire funeral process easier than it could have been. I was surrounded by my family and friends. They helped me select the plaque and casket. I had my mother, father, and best friend Meyuna to lean on every step of the way.

THE DAY I BURIED MY HUSBAND

I remember dreading the day of my husband's funeral. I didn't want it to happen, but on April 17, 2014, it did. It was one of the most disturbing and painful days of my life. I remember looking for a hat to go with what I was wearing because I didn't want anyone looking into my eyes. I did not want to face the stares of people there to see what I looked like or peering at me to see how I handled my emotions. I woke up that day, wishing that the fact Jermaine was gone wasn't true.

The sky was cloudy and drizzled rain. The weather really emphasized my mood. I remember sitting in my room when the driver came in and got me. I really didn't want to leave that room. If I stayed there, I could shut everything out. However, my driver would not give me the satisfaction. She told me, "Come on, baby girl. We have to do this."

It was in that moment that I knew that I could no longer hide as I had done for days leading up to the funeral. As we drove to the church, there was dead silence. No one talked. The mood was clearly somber. My heart began to race because I truly did not know what to expect. At the entrance to the church, I saw two fire trucks holding up the American flag as a symbol of respect and recognition to my deceased husband.

When we got out of the car, we waited until the video created to capture highlights in his life was over. It felt as though it took a life-time to get into the sanctuary. The only thing I remember is seeing Jermaine's casket and realizing that everything was indeed real. There was no turning back. My mind went numb when I told myself, "He will not come back. I have to accept my new reality." I walked up to the casket and tilted my head so that I could kiss Jermaine's forehead. That was my husband! I walked back to him again. This time, I kissed him three time because he told me that three was a sign of good luck. As I returned to my seat, I felt the weight of apprehension and dread momentarily lift off me. One of the hardest things I had ever done was over. Yet I knew that this was only the beginning of my pain. What I didn't know is that it would come and go without warning.

Something surprised me the day we buried Jermaine. I was touched by the people who came. It was truly amazing seeing my friends and Jermaine's friends from Lakeside and Morehouse College. I never knew how much he was loved until I saw all of the people that we hadn't talked to in years. It was the most encouraging feeling. For one brief moment, I didn't feel alone. It warmed my heart to see Jermaine's best friend speak at the funeral, because he literally stepped up to the plate and embraced me with true friendship. I know that Jermaine would have been so happy to see that. I also knew it would make Jermaine happy to know that his brothers and sisters from Firehouse Station 29 spoke tearfully about the good experiences they had with him. Whether it was about him cooking, telling jokes, or just being the kind-hearted person I've always known, their tributes to him were sincere and wonderful. They all made Jermaine sound like an angel who walked the earth.

Though I appreciated the true and authentic love that I received from family and friends, this day maximized my anxiety. I have never talked about it. But anyone who lives through this has to be prepared for the emotional struggles that come with burying your mate at a young age. I was on the verge of walking out of the sanctuary because I honestly felt like I couldn't breathe. It was just horrible, horrible, horrible. I really thought I was going to fall out and die. My chest hurt, and I could barely keep my composure.

The only way I got through it was to keep talking to myself. I kept saying over and over again, "This will pass. Everything is going to be fine." It was the first of many lies. However, I knew that this was also the beginning of having all the pain in my heart begin to bubble to the surface. What I didn't know was how deep that pain really was, how many areas of my life it would affect, and what part grief would play to slow my healing process.

MEMORIES

2

On what should have been my one-year wedding anniversary, I realized you can't move forward looking through a rear-view mirror.

Tanisha A. Hall

MEMORIES
@SIX MONTHS

October 12th marked the sixth-month anniversary of my husband not being here. However, October 12 would also have marked our one-year anniversary if he had lived. Early that day, my siblings and I went to a restaurant. I really enjoyed spending time with my brothers. When we were young, we argued and fought. Now, it's like we can't be separated. Nothing can break the bond we have. My brothers are always looking out for me. They are always trying to figure out every little detail for me! It reassures me that family is all you have when others are gone. Needless to say, I really needed to get out and do something and remember the love that Jermaine and I shared. If he were here, he probably would be at work, and later we would go to the movies or spend quality time at home. I'm not going to lie, we were homebodies, and to be honest, I didn't mind being at home. With that being said, I decided to go to church and go to lunch with my family. It was so refreshing to remember what love is all about.

Over the past few days, I've given a lot of thought to how my life has transformed. Though it's not what I want to be, I'm where I am supposed to be. My outlook on life is being changed daily to a more positive mindset. I no longer wish to sit and sob. I no longer want to join in on activities that don't hold my interest. I am growing and changing. I am beginning to do what makes me happy. And to be honest, life has been way more interesting than I could have ever thought. If I could change things, I would. If I could, I would bring Jermaine back.

But if I keep holding on to the impossible, there would be no possibility for a brighter future. Progress is not made with a rear-view mirror, and with that thought I can say, "Happy Anniversary to me and my loving husband."

Tanisha A. Hall

MEMORIES

3

Memories have to be managed and carefully selected – specifically on important dates like birthdays.

Tanisha A. Hall

MEMORIES
@ONE YEAR

The really sad thing about memories and grief are special dates. I had expected to have a life full of celebrating birthdays with my husband. I never got to celebrate any.

His birthday was in September. When I first decided to write this book, I really wanted to salute his memory by releasing it on his birthday or the anniversary of his death. Book writing is more work than I expected. I missed the date. When it became clear that was not going to happen, one of my brothers asked me a question I had never considered. "Why do you want to remember the day he died? That is nothing to celebrate."

The truth is I wanted to do something special, and remembering his death date is hard.

Every year when Jermaine's birthday or anniversary death date comes and goes, I don't know how to act. It reminds me that I miss my best friend. I miss seeing him and just giving him random kisses and hugs. I miss the opportunity of letting him know how much I truly care. Cared. I want this book to encourage all couples in love to cherish each other. Love your mate beyond your ups and downs. Be there for your loved ones no matter what. I will forever remember the moments we shared together. I love that he loved me in spite of my faults. So on Jermaine's birthday, I sit in the house we once shared together and tell him happy birthday – sometimes in tears.

But I don't let my hurt control my thoughts.

Instead, I try to remember how good we were together. Jermaine and I built our relationship on communication. I miss the days that we would talk randomly about whatever. I also miss the moments where we just did random things around the house like play hide-and-go-seek in the dark. We were young, right? I'm still young, and it makes me smile to think about those times. That moment makes me think about the love we shared.

Positive memories can go a long way toward healing a hurting heart.

Tanisha A. Hall

MEMORIES

4

Wisdom from a 24-year-old man.

Tanisha A. Hall

MEMORIES
@TWO YEARS

My memories are different now. I've moved away from the grief-obsessed mental turmoil that almost made me feel crazy. Yes, there are things I will never forgot that are negative. But each day I develop a stronger ability to remember the good times and see, through the eyes of experience, lessons I didn't understand before.

My late husband already knew these things. I look back in wonder and try to understand how the man I was married to for only six months could be so wise at age twenty-four. How could he understand that life is a mystery that can only be experienced and yet never solved?

There's one memory that makes me smile because it so clearly shows how well he understood the nature of time. He and I were thinking about having a BBQ at our house. I couldn't wait to start the preparations.

But my husband kept telling me to wait, be patient, and get closer to the date. One thing about my husband was that he always wanted me to wait and be patient. He was never a person to rush time and life. He lived in the moment and never felt the need to rush any decision. The more that I think about the things he told me, the more I realize that he lived more according to the spirit than the flesh. I understand that more now. Before, I never realized how life can bring you a different outlook or perspective almost instantly.

Life is about exploring, enjoying, and creating memories. I was so stuck on the future that I never realized my 'now.' I never knew that Jermaine would be my husband for only a few months. I was too concerned with inviting friends over to our house so that we could be wonderful hosts. I was excited about the get-together. We rarely had them for anyone other than family.

But now, two years later, reality has struck me so deep that it's hard to remember the words my husband told me: "Wait, be patient, let it happen." I truly believe that life has a way of teaching us patience regardless if you like it or not. Remaining humble was always easy but, patience? That was so hard for me. I'm learning now in this new beginning of my life to be patient. I have a new outlook on life, family, and love. I've learned to love them like never before. I've also learned how to not be so uptight about anything.

Trust me, if it's meant to happen it will. Accept disappointment. Disappointment to me is just another form of patience. I have concluded that when things happen in life or when things don't go as planned, then it was not meant to happen at that moment in your life. I've learned to let things be what they are.
 In regards to family, you may not approve of everything that they do, but accept them for who they are. My mom would always say, "People are going to be people." Just because you wouldn't do something to an individual does not mean they won't do it to you. People don't perceive things the same. If we did, we would be robots. It's okay; love them and keep it moving. In the past, I had let certain situations shake me to the point where my health was clearly affected (i.e., headaches and chest pain.) I am learning how to be more accepting of people.

We are all vessels. As people, we have to learn that living a good life takes time, growth, and honesty. Those three principles are very important to have. If we don't have time, then things would not be how we imagined. If we don't grow, we would not be able to accept the many possibilities that life has to present. Without honesty, we have nothing to stand for or offer. We also wouldn't be able to be trusted with other adventures and blessings.

Different stages of life bring new outlooks on many things. I've learned that it's important to be in tune to the many stages we are in. It's also important that when we are in these stages, we must learn to accept the new lesson. If we don't accept the stages, then we will repeat the same cycle. I know one thing for sure: I am willing to accept the point where I am in life. Each season teaches a different lesson, and every season brings a new beginning and outlook with it. The moment we realize that, that is the moment that we truly begin to grow and understand the power of memories in the healing process.

Tanisha A. Hall

JEALOUSY

1

I was either numb or bitter every waking moment.

Tanisha A. Hall

JEALOUSY
@30 DAYS

I had two emotions for thirty days after I buried my husband. I was numb and I was very, very angry.

All I could think about was the marriage I didn't have because my husband had passed. My thoughts were all negative, all the time. They told me I would never be a mother and other lies repeatedly. I couldn't stop them from rambling through my head. I ached and cried all the time. I didn't want to be around people who moved through the seasons of their lives without having grief beat them down. In other words, grief made me a very jealous person.

Prayer didn't even work. My prayers were silent rants about the injustice in my life. When I tried to pray for married couples, tears would just run down my face.
I was bitter. Now I know it was bitterness born by grief. Any little thing can set you off. I was set off a lot.

"Why is she even married, God? She is not pretty and doesn't even know how to dress."
"Why am I still single?"

"Why is this lady even pregnant?! She is not married."
But a lot of my jealousy was tied to the doubts I had about my own future.
People kept telling me that happiness was a choice. But for some reason, it felt as if my happiness and or even a glimpse of hope had been taken away. All I that I saw in my life was what I never wanted. I never wanted to write about the miseries of life and why

I was mad at God. I never wanted to talk about the anger that I have towards anyone because I know that I am not inherently mad. I want to know if my future will ever be brighter than my past. I oftentimes wonder if I will ever be a mother and wife. I wonder if God truly does exist and better yet, does He have my back? Then right behind the doubt, the jealous thoughts kick in.

As the ink dries on someone's marriage license, I hope it never works. I hope that the person one day will feel my pain. I know it may sound cold-hearted and mean but no one truly gets it. It doesn't feel good to be young and a widow. It doesn't feel good to be categorized as something that you never thought would happen until seventy years of age. So, to say that I had doubts would be an understatement. I had no clue as to what was going to happen next. I was trying to focus on the future, but my past hurt kept reminding me of what I had lost.

When I watched friends get married during this time, I felt persecuted. Why was this happening to me? I tried to be happy for other people, but in the beginning, it was too much of a struggle, and I lost all the battles against the jealousy-infused grief that I tried to fight. I missed my husband. I was becoming a different person without him, and that person wasn't nice.

Numbness and pain. Pain and numbness were all I remember about grieving during that first thirty days. The jealousy was on top of everything else, and it took time for me to understand how destructive it was in my life and how effectively it was blocking my ability to walk away from grief.

Licensed clinical psychologist and professional counselor
Shaneka McClarty LPC, NCC
Baltimore, MD

People will tell me they don't 'feel normal' while grieving. They shouldn't. Those who grieve have had a major shift and change in their lives. Not only are their hearts affected, but their souls are, too. If you are grieving, your world is not the same anymore. People who are around those who grieve have to acknowledge and accept that.

Of course, there are different types of grief. There are the therapists' ideal stages. But what we must remember is we shouldn't judge anyone because they're not grieving the way WE think they should grieve.

Tanisha A. Hall

JEALOUSY

2

*An ugly, public outburst finally exposed
the depth of my pain to my family.*

Tanisha A. Hall

JEALOUSY
@SIX MONTHS

On August 10th, three months after we buried my husband, I erupted in a way I never had done before in public.

Now in hindsight, I know it was the rawness of grief that had left me unprepared for interacting with the rest of the world. But two things made the incident worse. First, I had spent most of the day living inside my head. As a result, my feelings controlled my actions. I hadn't told anybody so when my parents, cousin, and brother all went on a boat ride, no one understood how emotionally fragile I was. They found out during a really festive group event where the announcer called out people who were celebrating anniversaries. It hit me like a rock. I kept telling myself, "Just get through this, Tanisha."

Then it went downhill. The announcer started going through the entire room asking everyone their last names and how long they had been married. Of course, there were a handful of people who were celebrating their weddings.

That broke me. I literally burst into tears. I told myself, "It can't get worse than this." It did, because then the announcer asked every married couple to stand up and come to the dance floor. I started mouthing curses. I didn't care; it was how I felt. I was with my family, and none of them had ever heard me say these types of things before. My emotional outburst shocked my Mom.

She looked at me and said, "Tanisha, why would you say that?"
As I look back, I know it hurt her to see me hurting. She couldn't fix it. She didn't under-

stand where the pain came from, and in her mind, I guess I was supposed to just suck it up and go on with life.

That's not how it seemed from my point of view, though. I was falling apart, and no one seemed to care. In fact, the people who knew me the longest and cared for me deeply had inadvertently put me in one of the most painful public situations I could have imagined. The boat ride exposed how raw I really was.

So, when I erupted in front of everyone, I wanted to be heard. I wanted everyone to feel my hurt and my pain. I became the type of person no one wanted to be seen with on that boat ride. But it didn't stop there.

Grief possessed me, remember?

I finally spoke the question out loud at the table that had been tearing me apart. "How can this couple be alive and Jermaine not be here with me?" I said loudly. No one comforted me because no one understood my grief and the ugly face of jealousy that it displayed.

But I was being honest. I really didn't understand why I hurt so badly, deeply, and often. And yes, I spewed my vicious comments while the celebratory couple was next to me. I had created an uncomfortable, public, and nasty situation. The problem was, I hadn't done it to be mean. I needed help. I wasn't getting it. What I got was my brother looking at me and saying bluntly, "Tanisha, that's not right."

That's not what I wanted to hear so I told him just as bluntly, "I don't care." Grief had complete control of me that day, and no one's feelings mattered but my own. It was all about me, me, and me. Actually, it was me and my grief. I hurt and that's all I knew.

It may not sound like it, but I'm a woman of faith, and I had been raised to 'cast all my cares.' Well, that didn't work, and the fact of the matter was, I just couldn't handle that particular situation. I now believe that I should not have had to live through it because I had already been told that grieving could cause individuals to have the type of outburst I had just forced everyone to witness.

The only good thing that came from that day is that I took ownership of what came from my mouth, and my family now knew my pain was real. A part of me was seething with anger. Another part of me was trying to move on. But I felt lost to the point where I didn't know how to get back to the person I used to be. I had never felt so broken and hurt at the same time. I went off that day because I just didn't know what to do with those feelings. I didn't know what to do about my grief.

I feel bad about my actions on that boat. I have repented. But back then, the only solution I could see was to not give up. I called on my best friend, God. Though I felt lost after my outburst on the boat, His word was a source of comfort for me. It was something that was part of my emotional development even before my husband passed.

So after the boat ride, I decided to keep that faith no matter how hard it was. I learned that we are all given tools to get through the storm. I just had to find mine. If you are reading this and grieving, know that you have to find yours. I was in no way perfect and am not so now. I will never be perfect, and you should not expect yourself to be, either. You can only trust that it will get better. I did not lose hope, even though I fell apart on the boat that day. But since that time, I've been able to get up.

The important thing to remember about my outburst and this story is that people consumed by grief should not be expected to control themselves in all situations. Be compassionate if you can when you see them fall apart. If they have what seems like an unreasonable reaction less than six months after someone has lost a piece of their heart- be patient. Grief has control of their emotions.

Licensed clinical psychologist and professional counselor
Shaneka McClarty LPC, NCC
Baltimore, MD

Some people bounce back and forth between denial and anger as they grieve. They can go back and forth with that for like months. What they should know is that grieving is a process. Even when you think you've come through it, you'll have these triggers. You'll have a holiday that will come up or you'll hear a song or you'll see someone who will remind you of that person. You may hear someone who sounds like that person. These are all triggers. So it's always a journey.

Tanisha A. Hall

JEALOUSY

3

I had to stop thinking about myself all of the time.

Tanisha A. Hall

JEALOUSY
@ONE YEAR

I cannot speak for anyone else, but even though I've lived without my husband for one year, I find it hard to rejoice with others. I found it very hard to be truly genuine with others when they were getting married, having a baby, or excelling in life (by my definition) happily. One year after I buried my husband, there were days when I wanted to rejoice with people doing these things, but my pain hindered me from truly doing something as simple as smiling authentically. I learned to fake it.

When I hurt or was crying inside, I overemphasized my smile. I knew some people looked at me and knew I was having a tough time. My smile, in those moments, wasn't sincere because I was trying to just get through it. Still, I learned to push past it.

Yes, I was twenty-four when I lost my husband. But what could I possibly do to bring him back? Absolutely nothing. So the question I had to ask myself was what could I do to help myself get through this traumatic experience? For me, the answer was to lean on God. There was also another support system. I tried to find things to do to that would take pressure off me and prevent me from living inside my head. At that time, I was just beginning to realize that losing something can bring out selfish tendencies. You don't know where they originate. They may have been learned or might have already existed. I don't know. I do know I tried to fight them because selfishness was tied to grief, and I wanted my grief gone.

At first, I just avoided events that I knew would hurt me. I received several invitations to attend weddings or engagement parties. I turned them down for the first year. But that got old. I just got tired of not being able to live my own life. I knew I couldn't continue living a life of avoidance. Do you know what I figured out? Other people's situations had nothing to do with my grief. I couldn't place blame on outside events. I had to stop expecting other people to treat me gently all of the time. That didn't help me. I've lived like my pain and hurt were the only things that truly mattered. The fact is, though, life goes on.

People are not going to constantly soothe a wound that can only be healed through a desire to get better. I had to stop wallowing in my pain, hoping that no one else got married and or had children. I didn't want to be selfish and only think about me, me, and more of me. This time in my life, at age 26 in 2015, I took a stand and refused to be selfish. I refused to stop thinking about my life as a young widow and, at the same time, wanting life to just freeze for everybody else. I finally figured out that if I truly wanted to heal, I had to stop thinking about myself all the time. Then, I made the decision to take the next step in my self-healing process.

A few years ago, mid 2015, I made a vow to the face I saw in the mirror that I was not going to run away from any situation. I was not going to run away from rejoicing with others. I was not going to let the tears run down my face publicly. But I also wasn't going to let one moment in time ruin my ENTIRE life. I was not going to allow the LIFE experiences of other people keep me in a perpetual state of sadness. I knew I couldn't heal if I remained stagnant. That hadn't been an easy decision to reach because the previous twelve months had been a hard season for me.

But one year after my husband passed, I learned something. I knew that we all face seasons of disappointment, contentment, and happiness. But these seasons don't last forever.

My fight with grief has finally reached a stage that has made me sensitive to other people. It is hard to smile through the hurt because it APPEARS that everyone around me has moved along. However, there is always someone going through some type of situation, whether they talk about it or not. We as individuals may not experience the same thing, but we darn sure are going through life. Remember that. The life you lead may not be what you want it to be but be grateful for it anyway. It takes time to reach that level of acceptance. But I'm here, and now I'm learning to pray for everything and everybody, even when it's the last thing I want to do.

Tanisha A. Hall

Licensed clinical psychologist and professional counselor
Shaneka McClarty LPC, NCC
Baltimore, MD

The only thing that the griever needs is your support, and that's it. You don't get to determine what that support looks like; only they can share that with you. And if they don't know what they need or they don't know right then, be patient. In many communities, people are there as soon as someone dies. We bring food. We show up to the wake, the funeral, and then days later – no one is there. Everyone disappears. But it's in those lonely hours that those who grieve need friends and family the most.

Tanisha A. Hall

JEALOUSY

4

*If I can't rejoice with others,
how can I expect joy in my life?*

Tanisha A. Hall

JEALOUSY
@TWO YEARS

Happiness is a choice. Each day, we choose to dwell in either misery or joy. Each day, we have the choice to be free from negative thinking or allow it to become our identity. There is so much more to life than disappointment or acting out because we do not get what we want, when we want it.

The more that I live, the more I believe that we are placed exactly where we need to be. We are in the right place, at the right time no matter how good or bad the situation may be. I once heard a minister say, "God did not answer the many prayers to get me out of a situation. He was using my situation to help another person." That's where I found myself in my journey of walking away from grief two years after my husband passed away.

In 2016, I decided that I was going to stop being sad and depressed about my life. Now mind you, I had spent the previous year making good on my vow of not wishing bad on folks who had all the things I had always wanted.

Now, I just stepped up my mental game. I made a simple choice that I was going to pray for people getting married and having children. I was even going to pray for people who had just started to date. Yes, I was still grieving, but I was no longer 'overcome by grief.' My mind was changing. My new thinking asked this question, "If I cannot rejoice with other people, then how on earth can I expect joy in my life?" I wanted to be used as an instrument to help others with similar situations. When I lived in a moment of pain, it felt as if God had abandoned me. That wasn't the case, just my perception of it. Two years after I buried my husband, I learned how to seek support from others. It didn't always work out. But one minister helped me find the tools that I needed to survive along with seeking counseling. I now believed I survived to help someone else. Yes, I had reached a new level of healing. I was learning that in the midst of every situation, it was possible to be happy and cheerful and to smile. That's a long way from how I felt six months after I became a widow. But two years later I slowly began to see happiness as a decision I could make no matter what events were going on in my life. I began to understand that happiness can exist during both dark and bright moments in life.

No situation or event should permanently ruin you emotionally. You can't live your life based on events. If you did, you would always be unstable and changing like the seasons. The challenge for me, that I want you to issue to yourself, is to learn the process of being happy that isn't dependent on some random act. It is a tool you need to conquer grief.

Then – don't berate yourself when something happens that makes you slide back into the pity pit.

We are all in the same race of learning how to trust a higher power. However, we run the same part of that race during different seasons of our lives. In my season of favor, winter, blessings did not fall at the same rate as they did for someone in the spring of life.

Winter for me brought the bright light of self-enlightenment. It showed me something I didn't like. I had developed self-righteous behavior, and what's really sad is that I had no idea what I was doing. I had talked myself into believing that I was better than other people. I thought that I had earned righteousness. I believed that since I did things that I had been taught to think of as 'right', God was going to bless me. I now know it doesn't work that way. Yes, I have also taken losses in this life that I may never understand. However, I am gaining knowledge. I never realized that because I have been blessed with good looks that I expected favor. It was pretty humiliating to see that, in my mind, I thought I should be married because I was beautiful. It's a realization I might never have had if grief had not beaten me down.

Now I know that I cannot look upon someone else and say that God should bless me the same way He has blessed them. We're operating in different seasons. However, two years after my husband passed away suddenly, I was convinced that God blesses people within their OWN seasons.

I have learned to trust and believe in the process of healing that can override grief. I also have learned to understand more about the seasons of life. Self-righteous behavior will not help me reach the level of spiritual development that I want to achieve. Self-righteous behavior leads to jealousy and envy. I've had enough of both.

If we truly want our lives to help others, we have to destroy self-righteous behavior. It hinders our blessings. Remove the 'better than thou' attitude and replace it with love and compassion. You'll be surprised at the effect doing so will have on your grief.

All of us have flaws. Take this time to really see those that exist within you and decide to deal with them before they gain too much control in your life.

Tanisha A. Hall

FORGIVENESS

1

Throughout the grieving process,
you'll become several different people.

Tanisha A. Hall

FORGIVENESS
@THIRTY DAYS

Grief will strip you bare of illusions about yourself. It's a humbling process. But when it's completed, you'll know more about who you are. You'll also see why some of the things you believed about yourself are actually not true. Throughout the grieving process, you'll become several different people. Some of them you do not like.

That's the point where forgiveness comes in. You have to look at people for who they are and not who you want them to be. People includes you. You'll have to change how you judge yourself. Grief makes it really hard to get a grip on who that really is. It's certainly not something you can do thirty days after you lose the person you love.

Forgiveness is not a platitude. It's a conscious act that first means you have to identify what is wrong. When you live a life without grief, wrongs are easy to identify. After grief sets up residence in your life, it's more difficult because you start to see everything differently. I really should say that you don't see things clearly. Everything is filtered through a gauze of pain. Thirty days into your struggle with grief you won't know that – which makes any type of forgiveness a little farfetched. You can't forgive what you don't understand, and that starts with yourself. You're changing and so is your relationship to other people. Get a handle on that before you start judging yourself or anybody else for a lack of forgiveness.

Tanisha A. Hall

FORGIVENESS

2

*What I learned about forgiveness
as a child was wrong.*

Tanisha A. Hall

FORGIVENESS
@SIX MONTHS

After spending six months feeling almost numb, I began to start noticing people around me again. I had a good friend who stepped into the gap, parents who loved me, brothers who would do anything to help me, and the support of my church.

None of that was good enough for me, because I was racked by pain, and it clouded my thinking. A lot of people got on my 'you have offended me' list two months after I buried my husband, Jermaine. I was just hurt and disappointed with their actions, because in my mind, they weren't treating me the way I wanted to be treated.

I was at a point where I did not want to talk to or even associate myself with certain individuals. It was so bad that I blocked phone calls. I completely convinced myself that I was forgiving but still talked about the people who wronged me, which included my friends and family.

However, the truth was -the problem was really me. I still filtered everything through not having my husband. I didn't even realize I was doing it until I heard a sermon about we only listen to things we agree with. That described me.

It was hard to not live in the past. I had to stop looking back so that I could look ahead. My goal was to focus on living in the present and look expectantly to the future. But I was also emotionally raw.

People being people was really more than I could take sometimes. But I knew I had to learn to get over it. I forgave an individual who hurt me. But the honest truth was when

I apologized I expected reciprocity. Later, I realized I wasn't ready to let go of all the hurt this person caused me. Well, that really isn't being forgiving, is it?

In fact, I sometimes wished that this person would feel the same hurt I felt.
I even wished that I could punish him. But what I felt was just plain wrong, and I knew it. I had to hold a mirror up to myself to understand that other people are not going to be judged because of what we do. They are going to be judged because of what they do. So was I. However, it was insincere to give an apology because I wanted one in return.

I think as little kids we were trained to say the words "I'm sorry," when we have wronged others. In life as adults, it doesn't always work like that, when I really start to think about it.
I truly think that when we show more love than pain, we begin to heal. Of course, it takes time, and six months after a life tragedy wasn't long enough. At least, I now know it wasn't long enough for me. It took more time for me to see life's funny way of showing us things. It took months before I could accept things the way they were, not the way I wanted them to be. I guess it was part of the maturing process. The more mature I become, the more I begin to learn to let things go. It was another step in my ability to battle grief.

The lesson at this period in my life was to be honest and admit when I was wrong all while being honest about my feelings. I had to stop deceiving people, and myself, into believing something that is not true. I would smile, hug, and even talk to people. In the back of my mind, though, I pondered thoughts that were not pure. I truly believe that maturity brings about honesty, character, and so much more. My desire every single day is to do more things right than I do wrong and do a better job of making sure all of my actions are based in love.

FORGIVENESS

3

You can't forgive anyone until you forgive yourself.

Tanisha A. Hall

FORGIVENESS
@ONE YEAR

We ask others to forgive us, but do we ever forgive ourselves? This is a great question to think about. Over these past few months, I have allowed myself to be beat up inside. I have beaten myself up over guilt, hurt, shame, and disappointment.

For one, I have on several occasions blamed myself for my husband's death. Wow, I never thought that I would admit that out in the open. But, I just did. I would replay the things I said, how I acted, just everything, and I would do it daily. I would think, if I would have done this, that or whatever, then he would be here and alive. Then I have to remember it wasn't my fault. I could not control what happened to him.

I felt I was not a good enough wife so maybe I deserved to be a widow. I mean, I wasn't a perfect person. Who is? Before the grief of losing him made me more compassionate, I used to let any and everything set me off. I would also let any and everything come out of my mouth.

So yes, I felt like God was punishing me. I felt like God was saying, "Since you cannot be compassionate, I'm going to smack compassion into you." It made sense to me. When I shared my thoughts with my Mom, she set me straight. "God does not operate like that," she told me. What she said gave me a moment of peace. I may have nagged my husband here and there, but that didn't mean I deserved to walk around hanging my head with guilt.

Yes, both guilt and grief had strong holds on me. I was also ashamed. I used to walk around with my head down because I did not want to be labeled. I refused to be that girl, the widow. It was so bad that I would try to hide my face everywhere I went. I just felt ashamed because of what happened to me.

How could I say that God is love when I didn't love myself? For a while, that meant I did nothing to take care of myself. Now I've started doing something different. I make sure I dress nicely, get my hair done weekly, and keep my nails up. That's a big deal because for months I stayed in bed and watched TV. I didn't want to make friends. I didn't want to see people.

It took several months for me to realize that hiding my hurt, disappointment, and shame didn't help heal the hurt. See, I found out that I could control my exterior but not what I felt. But that is changing. I'm learning each day to love me, love Neno/Tanisha (as Jermaine used to call me.)

Take what I'm writing and apply it to your own life. You can't forgive anyone until you forgive yourself. In order to give love, you have to love yourself. I challenge you, love yourself. Embrace yourself. Stop blaming yourself. Start the whole process with forgiving YOURSELF!!!!!!

Tanisha A. Hall

FORGIVENESS

4

This journey has taught me to look at life less traditionally.

Tanisha A. Hall

FORGIVENESS
@TWO YEARS

The older that I get, the more I realize that people do not mean any harm. It really took me a minute to get to that point. People do what they know and or think they know. They only go by their feelings and sometimes nothing else. For the longest time in my life, I always thought that people did things just to hurt me or to be vindictive. At times, that may be the case, but sometimes, people do things because they only go by what they want for themselves. I think society teaches us to focus on ourselves. Society has taught us as human beings to be selfish and treat people based on how we feel.

However, as Christians, we have been taught to show kindness to people who mistreat us.

Sometimes, we think that life is full of just one train of thought. But it is full of many things and modes. It has a way of showing us who we are, dictating what our life has transformed into, and everything else. We never expect certain things to happen in our lives. We never expect the downfalls that life brings because we have been sheltered, but once life shows us our true meaning, we begin to look at it and experience it so differently.

I have learned that life can be beautiful if you take the necessary steps to make it that way. We are all given the same opportunity, but we also have choices to make. However, the important thing is how we deal with the factors that life gives us all. As I am writing this, I noticed that my life has had disappointments and misunderstandings. However, one thing still remains the same: I will never give up. Somehow, I have strength that has been embedded deep inside me for the longest time. This strength was given to not only me, but to each and every one of us; we just have to tap into our capabilities.

My motto is that along with disappointment come strength and maturity. Along with frustration comes a fight, a fight to never give up. Along with tears come streams of joy knowing that there is a shift toward the truth. Of course, with growing, we have to be stretched. Of course, with stretching, we will experience pain. The pain will not last long. It's amazing how mothers, during the birthing process, experience pain. But when the baby arrives, it seems as if the pain and bloodshed all disappear. The only thing that matters is the baby. If mothers can go through excruciating pain with bliss and joy as the end result, why can't you and I do the same? Though our outcomes may be different, they still consist of the same results: pain, then beauty. No matter how tough it is, never give up. I have to tell myself that sometimes. If I'm still here by the Grace of God, so are you.

Make up in your mind; you can and will ride the tide. You are going through growing pains and you can make it through. Through the birthing process, you are learning, growing, and expanding on the experiences you face along the way.
As a new widow, I always wondered what my life would be like without Jermaine. I also at times ask myself, "Is this really true?" I know the answer; I'm just reminding myself that it is true. I don't know why things happen the way they happen. I really don't know why one is so happy to be married only to see it unexpectedly disappear. Then, life has a way of telling us the importance of love and life! Someone out in this world has also lost a wife, husband, and or loved one. For the longest time, I only thought it was about me and my loss, yet there are other people who are still hurting.

We all face some type of adversity whether through death, loss of job, etc. As humans, we are grieving some type of loss through life's journey. However, we must somehow find hope and strength through the journey. We must try to encourage ourselves in the midst of our ups and downs. When I got the news that Jermaine had no brain function, I was crushed. You know the dream you might have about one of your family members dying? Yeah, well, mine actually came true. I had no thought about the tough times my husband and I had faced. They no longer mattered. I just wanted him to come back to me. But the reality of it was, that couldn't happen. All I have is memories of him and me and the life we had built together. Why does it seem that when we get it together, piece by piece it all falls apart? Maybe it was not meant to be – I don't know. But somehow, some way, we must put the pieces back together with love, hope, and understanding.
 I have never faced adversity that has broken me to core like this one. I think it is safe to say that this moment in my life has truly impacted me the most. Out of all the things I have been through, I can honestly say this obstacle has questioned my belief and faith. When it all falls apart, maybe it is truly falling together. One thing that I took from this thing called life is that it loves you. It is not against you; it is just trying to show you

lessons. It is hard to believe when we are going through. But I believe that we can love again and move forward to being the best that we were created to be. Things may not be where and how you want them to be, but things will come back together.

Tanisha A. Hall

INTERACTIONS

Normal emotions are put on hold
when someone you love passes.

Tanisha A. Hall

INTERACTIONS
@30 DAYS

Friends occupy a new place in your heart and life when you lose a mate. I was lucky, even though I started shutting people out and not returning calls or texts from the hospital after Jermaine went into a coma. I couldn't deal with the constant reminders that something was truly wrong with Jermaine. I didn't want to face the fact that his life was really coming to an end, and the text messages I received were only confirmations of that. Besides, some of the people reaching out to us were folks I hadn't heard from in years.

One exception was from my BFF. I didn't want to talk to her, either. However, I decided to let her know the hospital where Jermaine was receiving treatment so that she could come and give support the best way she knew how. When I look back, I'm surprised how secure she made me feel. Just seeing her let me know I had someone to rely on. Her presence was a breath of fresh air that allowed me to relax and depend on her for strength. It was as if I was able to stand through the obstacle of being a widow more easily with her around.

She supported me even after the trauma at the hospital. She stayed with me for a month. What a blessing she was. I didn't have to be alone. We'd watch streaming movies all night so I could try to get my mind off how horribly my life had changed. She had just encountered a setback in her own life and had lost her job. But instead of focusing on getting another paycheck, she spent every second of her day with me. I had moved back in with my parents, and she seem to enjoy hanging around with all of us.

But then grief began to ravage me and my relationship with her. I began to resent her. Actually, I began to resent everybody. I didn't grieve during the funeral. The hardest part was after the funeral when the phone calls, home visits, messages begin to stop. That is when raw emotions like anger and disappointment begin to well up. Did I mention the anger?

I have never really acknowledged the individuals who came to the hospital during those early morning hours as Jermaine's life ebbed away. I can honestly say I wasn't in my right mind. I was in a state of grief. So here and now, I want to thank all of Jermaine's friends from middle and high school, close family members, the fire fighter family from Station 29, and a host of other individuals from the Atlanta Fire Department. Please know I sincerely appreciated your visits. Thinking about it now brings tears to my eyes that I was incapable of crying then. I never knew how much Jermaine was loved until seeing the numbers of people who showed up at the hospital that day.

Licensed clinical psychologist and professional counselor
Shaneka McClarty LPC, NCC
Baltimore, MD

It is important for friends and family to remember that grief does not stop after the funeral. The griever continues to struggle with the loss after the calls, visits, etc. stop. It is important to check in on the griever. Some people's grief can be displayed as what can be considered avoidance, being disconnected, running away. There are many stages of grief, and all can display themselves in different ways. Just as a note, I normally don't go to funerals. I'm the person who shows up after. I write a series of letters, perhaps six, and I schedule when I'm going to mail them out so that I'm always reaching out to the grieving person and talking to them and calling them. Because people still need you.

Tanisha A. Hall

INTERACTIONS

2

Why the "I'm sorry for your loss" speech doesn't help.

Tanisha A. Hall

INTERACTIONS
@SIX MONTHS

The grieving process turned me into a person I did not recognize six months after we buried Jermaine. I would ignore phone calls from individuals who wanted nothing more than to send love to me. I hated everything that resembled love, and I wanted everyone to know exactly how it felt. I didn't want to talk to anyone and I didn't want anyone to know what was going on with me. I had completely shut everyone out of my life. I had become more secretive than normal. For the most part, I always wanted to be alone. I wanted to soak in my misery, in my thoughts, and ignore the people who would not stop calling me. That included my wonderful BFF who had put her life on hold to help me heal.

"Tanisha, why aren't you answering my calls? Tanisha, where are you? Tanisha, are you okay?!" Those were the text messages that I would receive from her every day, and my torn, grieving heart was too callous to let me respond. Dealing with people was really a day-to-day thing with me.

At the end of six months, I forced myself to move forward. My relationships with family and friends were still fragile, but at least I wasn't staying at home all of the time. My anger was not out of control as much. I still hurt, but it seemed to be lessening. I'm not sure. My memories from that time are foggy. What I am sure of is I was getting a handle on my life. Or I thought I was until someone I had never met had to remind me.

"Tanisha, I am so sorry for your loss," this couple said sincerely. The last thing I wanted to do was meet 'new' people who knew my story and shoved it in my face. I dreaded the moments where I met people who greeted me with the "I'm sorry" speech. It's offensive to introduce yourself that way to anyone. Do you walk up to someone and say, "So sorry for your missing leg or acne scars or hair loss?" No, it would be considered rude.

The 'I'm sorry for your loss speech' was said to me a lot, and I didn't know how to cope with it. At one point, I really thought that I was better than the 'I'm sorry speech' until someone mentioned it to me not too long ago. My typical response is, "It's okay." I truly convinced myself that it was, but then I started really thinking about it.

The 'I'm sorry for your loss speech' makes me cry. I hate those words because every time I hear them I'm slapped with my new reality. It's only been six months. Those words remind me that my new reality is a life without Jermaine. My reality is that I am young, alone, and have to keep pushing.

Since we're talking about hurtful words, let me tell you others I hate hearing.
How about "You're young, you will find someone else." Those words really eat at me. Who are you to say that while I'm hurting? How dare you say I will find love again? I married my best friend and someone I'd been close to almost half my life. If I started a serious relationship right now, it would take me ten years just to get to the same point.

Yet, I know people say these phrases as an expression of true sympathy. I guess this is an area that I need to work on. I don't want to be this easily broken. I yearn for the day that I can meet people and be bold enough to tell my story.
Writing about my feelings is different. It's very therapeutic and encouraging. But talking about my story in person can be traumatic. It just shows the true power of words.

We all have areas that we have no control over. To be honest, we can overcome, though. My mindset has changed. If I can even have the audacity to write this, you can have the power to push through. There is no such thing as 'good grief' but it does come in many different forms.

What kind of grief are you dealing with? Face it. Fight it and win.

　　　　Tanisha A. Hall

Licensed clinical psychologist and professional counselor
Shaneka McClarty LPC, NCC
Baltimore, MD

People who are grieving need time to heal. They don't need you to ask, "How are you doing?" Because when you ask how they are doing, they're not going to tell you. Instead of a question, do more prompting. Make statements such as "Tell me what you've been thinking about lately" or "Tell me how you've been coping. Tell me what can I do. Let me know what you need." If the person is getting counseling, do not expect the counselor to heal grief. It can't be done. Nor will the grieving person feel better after one session or two or even the fourth, because it takes time to talk about the pain of grief. Those who grieve, and get counseling, should only talk about their loss when they're ready. The important thing to understand is that the therapist will not make you feel better; no one has the power to do that. The therapist will help everyone understand that grief is a journey, and everyone's journey is different.

Tanisha A. Hall

INTERACTIONS

*No one can put their life on hold
for you while you grieve.*

Tanisha A. Hall

INTERACTIONS
@ONE YEAR

The first year was the hardest for me. It was hard to believe that Jermaine wasn't alive. Every day that I woke up, I was reminded that he was no longer here. I had to continually tell myself that Jermaine had actually transitioned. For the longest time, it felt like I was in a dream and couldn't wake up. I was very numb and hated everyone who talked to me. I was upset with my mother, brothers, and anyone else who did not understand where I was coming from.

For people to sit and tell me that they understood me or compared losing a husband to divorce made me mad. It was one of many things that did. If I went out and I saw someone I knew, I would try my best to look the other way and/or walk the opposite direction. I made a hobby of changing my number, because too many people had it and actually called to check on me.

I was tired of talking to people, and I was tired of hearing people tell me that, "With time, things will get better." How would they know? They didn't even understand how horrible I felt. I was also angry with my best friend simply because she wouldn't put her life on hold for as long as I desired. I wanted her to be at my every beck and call, even though she had stayed with me an entire month. But that wasn't enough. I wanted more from her and my family. I wanted the constant reminders. Overall, I wanted the love from the people around me. But I wanted it at a level no one could humanly maintain.

However, it's hard to love someone who can't control their emotions, specifically in public. The strange thing about grief is its negative power digs so deep into your heart and thoughts that minor actions can cause major eruptions that no one, including the bereaved, predicts.

You might think you're in control of your life, but you can quickly be reminded that's not true.

I took time out with my family to go to Florida. It was very relaxing until people become nosy, wondering my age, if I had kids, and if I was married. Those questions are truly the most challenging and hurtful to answer at times. I know those people, of course, didn't know me. Why does the questioning hurt so much? Yes, I was married, and yes, I was working on having kids! As of now, I am single and finding my happiness again. My question is, why do people find a timeline for everything? I had a timeline to get married and have kids. Now, I'm just 25 and single with zero kids. Am I sad? Yes, sometimes. Do I miss being married? Of course.

There has to be some beauty behind my pain. There has to be some type of happiness beyond this tragic moment. I haven't seen it yet. One thing for sure, I'm not putting a timeline on my life anymore. Whatever detour happens in my life was meant to happen! I'm not saying that it won't initially be disappointing, but it surely will bring me to my destiny and purpose. I cannot change that I am a widow. What I can change is my outlook on my life and experiences. One thing that I have learned is that our timelines are never set in stone. What's planned has the option to be changed and or altered. My plan has changed. Does it feel great? No, Lord knows I do not like this pain. However, I have to embrace the place that I am at now before the next level in life. Things are not always going to be the way you want them to be. Embrace change and the unexpected!

Tanisha A. Hall

Licensed clinical psychologist and professional counselor
Shaneka McClarty LPC, NCC
Baltimore, MD

There's no such thing as a grief timetable. It's not how long I (as a therapist) think it should last. It varies for everybody. I've seen it last a few months. I've seen it last for year. It varies. I think when it becomes five years that I, as a clinician, consider it a change from grief to major depression. So, what a therapist might be concerned about is if you're ruminating over your loss two or three years later. This is not grief anymore. You're clinically depressed. Grief is the root part of it, the trigger for it. It is more likely to happen when the person who is grieving doesn't have good coping skills or a strong support system. But understand that long-term grieving can become depression even with support and the ability to work through the process.

Tanisha A. Hall

INTERACTIONS

4

Dating means not looking for an exact replica of Jermaine.

Tanisha A. Hall

INTERACTIONS
@TWO YEARS

Communication is one of the most important ways of coping with life. Everything that we do in my opinion is a form of communication whether it's verbal or nonverbal. We all have our own unique way of speaking to one another. Whether you like it or not, it is important to remember how we come across to people. No matter what, we must operate in love even when the person who is speaking with us doesn't.

There's still something I want everyone who reads these words to recognize. It takes time to absorb and live with the new reality of being a widow or widower. It took almost two years before I could interact with new and old acquaintances without having the urge to sock people in the face.

It took the same amount of time before I was able to meet new people or have conversations with old friends from high school.

I'm at least seeing how needy and dependent I have been and trying not to drain the people who have chosen to stay with me, people like my best friend.

Two years after my husband passed, I'm finally able to go out by myself without fear that someone will know my story. I guess that's one way of saying it's taken this long to get over the shame.

Tanisha A. Hall

FAITH:
MY BEST TOOL FOR FIGHTING GRIEF

I've come this far by faith, but I didn't lean on the Everlasting Arms the entire way.

FIGHTING GRIEF WITH FAITH: THE STARTING LINE

My faith in God wasn't tested by grief.

It was stomped, shattered, shredded, bounced off walls, flushed, and completely dis-regarded at times.
Was I mad at God?
Well, my husband of six months died unexpectedly from a brain aneurysm. We were both only 24 years old. I'll let you answer the question for yourself when you read what I have written. Understand that through it all, I was trying to cope with grief. This section of my book may shock some people. I'll be honest. The words I wrote and the feelings I had would have shocked me too before I lost my husband. Now I understand why it's impossible for one mere human to judge another. You have no idea how another person feels, and for that reason, you can't condemn their decisions.

I was raised in the Christian faith and wanted to believe that everything I read in the Bible and heard in church would heal all my hurt. It didn't. But that doesn't mean I stopped trying to be faithful.

What you will read in this section are the paths I took toward having a deeper spiritual life. For me, that meant growing closer to God through Jesus. But my path toward spir-itual growth isn't exclusionary, because I truly believe that God is love, and love has no limitations.

Faith and God were really important to me as I grieved. But there were times I was so angry I just didn't care about either. This section summarizes my battles and my growth. I learned how to see truth for myself, without framing it through the lens of someone else's vision. I urge you to find your own path toward spiritual healing as you work through the grief process. All of us are made of body, mind, and spirit, and true healing only takes place when all three receive salve.

Tanisha A. Hall

FIGHTING GRIEF WITH FAITH:
BITTERNESS 2014

I can't speak for anyone else but me. After my husband's funeral, I was bitter. I was angry with God. I did not want to have any part of worshipping a God who allowed me to be so broken. I was so torn up inside that all I would do is wake up and cry. I blamed God for my hurt and pain. I could not worship a God who I swore heard my cries, but did absolutely nothing to help me.

Those feelings didn't last. But they did make me think about the reasons I had faith in the first place. Some of them were false. We all say that we love God and He is so faithful. However, once adversity hits us, we question our beliefs. I began to check myself. I knew that God would not want anyone to hurt needlessly. But I could see no reason I was filled with pain.

FIGHTING GRIEF WITH FAITH:
HEY GOD? I DOUBT YOU 2014

I wonder if God truly does exist and even more, does He have my back? I have nothing but venom inside me, and it's directed at everything and everybody. That's how I feel.

I have no clue as to what will happen next. I am trying to focus on the future, but my past hurt keeps reminding me of what I have lost.
The doubts about my future appear much stronger than any new plan of my life. Right now, everything seems unreachable.
Got doubts? Yes, more than I ever thought were possible.

FIGHTING GRIEF WITH FAITH:
WHEN AM I GOING TO STOP HURTING? 2015

I am hurt, still.
I am still suffering in silence from the pain that I have. I have no clue as to why Jermaine was taken away from me. I wonder if Jermaine could have fought to maintain his existence on this earth?
How could it be that I am the only one in my circle of influence to have lost a spouse of only six months?
How could it be that I am twenty-six and trying to pick up the pieces that I thought were already set in place?
Shattered? Yes, I am. I am hurt from the pain in my life, still. I wonder sometimes, where is God in the midst of my struggle? Yes, I am still on "Where is God?"

But then when I don't get answers, I end up being angry with God because I truly cannot grasp this new concept in my life.
Out of all the people in the world, why me?
Not to mention His silent response to my questions and worries in this life. If I had the option to trade a life with someone, I would in a heartbeat. No questions asked.

Life is not what we think it is supposed to be, but do we deserve to still wallow in pain? Do we deserve to hurt constantly over yesterday's worry and fear? How do we somehow grasp onto the new concept in our life?

FIGHTING GRIEF WITH FAITH:
WHAT GOES IN COMES OUT 2015

Over the past few weeks, I have been listening to a sermon on speaking words of declaration and empowerment. I never knew that the more you listen to things, the more your faith is stirred up.

The Bible clearly states: faith comes by hearing and hearing by the word of God. We must be mindful of what we put in our heart and mind. We must know that everything we do does play a certain role in our life.

Could it be that we are listening to too much music that talks about depression, anger, and struggle? Or could the music tell us we don't have a certain body type, so we are not pretty enough? Could it be that we are watching shows that tell the story of a little girl who struggles with an addiction? The Bible states that our eyes are the gatekeepers to our souls.

What are we allowing our eyes to see that tells us who we are? Why must we feel validated by music, guys, girls, etc.? God clearly stated who we are in His word. He says we are the head and not the tail. He says we are above and never beneath. To take it another step further, He also promised us life and life more abundantly. He says that He will make our enemies our footstools. What more validation do we need?

In my opinion, insecurities are another form of bondage that try to hinder us from our destiny and purpose. We must be mindful of how we allow others to tell us who and what we are. We must be mindful that God's word is more than enough confirmation of who we are. If we learn to put our trust in Him, He will give us the desires of our heart and more than we can understand. He states that He will give us peace that surpasses all understanding. Here is a declaration that can be used any day or time.

Repeat: "I refuse to be insecure. I do not lack anything; God supplies all of my needs. I am strong in the Lord and in the power of His might. I won't be anxious or worried about anything, but in everything I give praise and make my request known to God. God's peace will keep and cover me."

FIGHTING GRIEF WITH FAITH:
GOD IS IN CONTROL 2015

December 09, 2015, I decided to stop looking at what I don't have, and focus on the possibilities. I'm nervous of course but am taking a leap of faith and pressing towards the many beautiful things that can inspire me.

I refuse to think about the negative when I know there are so many things that can help me get to where I truly would like to be. The depressing thoughts (Doubting Tanisha) always describe the worst case scenario. How many times does the worst case scenario ever arise? How many times does the worst thought ever truly manifest itself to the capacity that we believe it will?

Sometimes, we have to take a leap of faith and know that God is in control. We have to stop trying to place everything on what God can do for us. At some point, we have to take action and listen to the voice of the Lord for discernment and guidance. Life is not what we thought it was going to be. However, we have the choice to have faith or not. We have to move forward in life, knowing that God has us in the palm of His hand. There is more to life than the hurt and pain. There is more to life than what we see and or know. There is more to life than what we can ever think about or imagine.

Have faith, have hope, and believe that at some time it will be better.
Faith is not what we think will happen but what we believe will happen. What are you focusing on? What thwarts your beliefs and the plans that God has for you? I don't know about you, but I'm tired of allowing bondage and brokenness to be a part of my ministry and life.

The train of doubt, unbelief, and shame ends today. I left them and am riding on the train of infinite possibilities. When it feels like you haven't reached another level, keep pressing. When it feels as if you have nothing left, go to God in prayer.

Have faith and believe that there is something better no matter what the situation looks like.
Have faith!

FIGHTING GRIEF WITH FAITH:
A 'REAL' RELATIONSHIP 2016

My spiritual growth has caused me to look at two unsettling truths.
My relationship with God was a 'what can you do for me' type of thing. My attitude was, "Hey God, if You help me with this, I will praise You and go to church this Sunday." See, I failed to realize that God does not operate like that. He is a jealous God and wants the praise that He is due. That type of tit-for-tat belief kept me from growing in Christ. The older that I get, the more I realize how precious life is. I realize that God is the same. His word never changes or will return void. In order to help others, we must first grow and know the word for ourselves. We are examples to the world! How can we expect someone to believe in the only God if we live as if God is nothing? As harsh as that may sound, I know I didn't put my hope or anything else in God.

That's the first unpleasant truth. The next one caused me to shake my head. My hope was in my husband and what he and I had going on.

I am not sure why Jermaine is no longer here. What I do know is that I am growing in Christ daily. Before I start my day, I pray, read the word, and speak my affirmations! In order to grow in Christ, we have to feed our faith. Now, I'm not saying that your story toward spiritual growth is going to be the same as mine. You have to find your own salvation and journey. But the Bible I read says, "Choose this day whom you will serve."

I honestly and boldly can say I choose God. I just have to give myself a quick self-check to remember.

FIGHTING GRIEF WITH FAITH:
GIVING IT TO HIM? 2016

Give it to God. I know it's easier said than done, but we all have areas that we have no control over. So why not give it to God? I am so tired of trying to fight by myself when God said that He will fight for me and you. To be honest, we can overcome; if I can even have the audacity to write this, you can have the power to push through whatever faces you.

FIGHTING GRIEF WITH FAITH:
STRENGTH AND PAIN=POWER

As I was in my car, listening to music, a thought came to me which was clear as day on God's love. The thought was, "Can what I am going through be a reflection of God's love? How can God turn something so shameful into something so beautiful?" For over a year, I had the hardest time understanding pain being a mere reflection of God's love for me.

I did not comprehend how my messed-up situation could bring joy and truth without causing more hurt. However, I have learned that just because one bad event happened does not mean that God loves me any less. I think when we go through trials, we are so quick to jump ship on God. But when times are the way that we want, we are so honest in exclaiming our love for God. The beautiful thing about God is that He loves us in our mess, flaws, and pity parties. He loves us when we are wrong and even when we are right. His love for us never fails.

The golden key about God is that He somehow equips us with the strength to endure each setback. He equips us with the knowledge and wisdom to truly plug into Him. The pain that we go through in life may never be comprehensible. However, the love that God has for us outweighs the bad in our lives.

Think about a time when you never thought you would make it. Think about the mo-

Tanisha A. Hall

ments in which you were going to give in and what happened? You somehow were able to pull through. Although the pain may not reflect love at times, you have to continually reassure yourself that God loves you. God wants what's best for you. It may not feel like it, but we have to stop thinking about our feelings and believe for the best

FIGHTING GRIEF WITH FAITH:
GOD DID HIS PART. MY TURN NOW 2015

I am realizing that God did his part and now it is time for us (meaning you and me) to do ours.

We must fight back when it seems as if we have nothing left. Fight the emotions of fear, fight the emotions of doubt, fight the emotions of hurt. Every negative emotion is as strong as YOU make it. Every negative thought is as strong as YOU want it to be. Sometimes, we depend on God to do everything when he has given us the keys and tools. His word says that "Greater is He that is in YOU than He that is in the world."

Stop allowing negative thoughts to run havoc in your life.
Remove the fear and change your life. Fear is a strong emotion, but we are much stronger than the emotion. We have more power and strength than we think we do. Remember, the greater one is living inside of you. Rise up and know that you can do all things.

FIGHTING GRIEF WITH FAITH:
BROKEN AND BLESSED 2016

March 5, 2016, was my breaking point in which I was over trying to pretend.
There were times in which I forced myself to not be sad. There were also times I just wanted to remain angry. Then, a thought finally came to me: "Tanisha, are you truly upset or are you wanting the attention and concern of others? Do you really want to be whole from everything that has happened in your life? Or, do you want to continue and wallow in things that you cannot control?" The more I thought about it, the more I realized that I cannot sit in misery any longer.

For quite some time, I have been asking God to heal the broken pieces of my life. But how can He if I am too busy telling God all about my problems and pain? How can He heal the areas that left me broken when I keep reminding Him of what happened? I want to be whole, and I think sometimes the pain of my past brings comfort. I somehow have grown too comfortable with pain.

I am reminded that if I truly want to get my life back to where it needs to be, I need to just remain and be in the be. Meaning, I need to allow God to do what He does while I accept what I cannot undo and or change. My heart's desire is to accept the loss of what I do not have. In the process, I have to recognize that I am no longer living in what cannot be undone. Time has changed, along with my environment.

However, am I truly trusting that things will be different because I do not get what I want at the moment? Am I truly trusting God to make things great when I focus on the pieces that were from my past? NO!! In order to be whole, I have to truly trust God and wait in the process. I have to understand that I am capable of love, respect, and truth. I am beautiful, and I can be beautiful by myself.

If I truly want God to heal every area of my life, I have to remind Him and myself that He is all that I need. I do not need a man or relationship to bring joy into my life. I do not need a husband to bring true fulfilment. The thing about temporary gratifications are that they last only for a moment. But if I want to find joy and wholeness, I have to aim towards God. Does it hurt to know that where I want to be is not where I am? Yes. However, it is only for a moment. To truly be whole, I have to make steps of acceptance, peace, and love. So today, March 4, 2016, is the day that I accept the challenge to be and remain whole.

FIGHTING GRIEF WITH FAITH:
YOUR VERY BREATH IS A BLESSING

Never let your thoughts tell you that you cannot win and you are not enough.
I remember sitting in the hospital and listening to the news of Jermaine's fate. Everything in me was ready for battle and war for him. I never wanted to give up. I somehow had faith built in me from the years of attending church as a little girl. That same warrior mentality that I had must be applied after everyone has moved on with their lives a year later. Every bone and fiber within you has to know that you are better than what you think. You are better than what you feel. You are better than what you see. You are created perfectly for such a time as this.
Each day that you are given breath is another moment to fight.

You have exactly what it takes. You know what to do even when it does not feel like it.

FIGHTING GRIEF WITH FAITH:
GIVING AWAY THE MEMORIES OF MY PAST

Two years ago, I was a wife, believing God to be a mother.
In believing God, I started to prepare myself. Jermaine and I decided to decorate the babies' room (I wanted a two for one deal: twins.) I also decided to go to Babies R' Us and buy my twins' clothing.
For some reason, I had the faith knowing that I was going to be a mother. So, in my mind, I had to take action in order to activate my faith. Fast forward one year later.

It's 2015. My husband has been in a grave for a year, and I have been feeling a tug on my heart to give away the baby clothes. For quite some time, I have used the baby clothes as a vision for myself.

Tanisha A. Hall

However, I know that I need to focus, and my desires will fall in line later. Until then, I can truly be a blessing to some other married couple. It took me a long time to make this decision. In order to receive more, I have to be able to willingly give. I am learning through this process that everything is not just about my pain and/or hurt. There are others who need to see Jesus through small gestures and words.

FIGHTING GRIEF WITH FAITH:
EQUIPPED TO WIN IN EVERY SEASON 2014

My best friend made a statement that astonished me. She said, "We should accept our reality and thank God for it."

At that moment, I did not want to hear it; I just could not deal with God putting me through struggle. The only way to be driven to our purpose is through struggle. Before my husband passed, I hardly ever wrote, I hardly ever prayed or meditated on God's words.

It was because of my struggle that I started to write, pray, and meditate. Clearly, I have been driven to God. I know that God has a plan that has not been aligned with my plans. His word states that His thoughts and plans are not the same as ours. Therefore, what I think I should go through is not what God thinks I am capable of going through.

My prayer is that through every season, the Holy Spirit equips me with tools for the journey. I don't understand why I am a widow at age 25. What I do know is that God has graced you and me through whatever season we're in. Although it may feel as if we are in the winter season, I do believe that God is giving us grace and strength to get to the sunshine.

Whom the Son sets free is free indeed. I look at that Bible verse as the sun coming out and releasing hope, strength, beauty, and grace. God says He will give beauty for ashes. We have to believe our season has been meant for change, change to grow into the individual we are meant to be in life. Each season is meant for purpose, purpose to grow and become the true person we have hidden inside of us. Each day, I thank God for the anointing on my life to lead and guide me.

As we grow, we must change. Each season is different; each story is different. How are you going to handle them? I don't know about you, but, I've decided to let God have His way with my life. I refuse to plan and get upset with God when it doesn't go as I wanted. Therefore, I accept each and every season, knowing that God can and will bring us through as VICTORIOUS!

FIGHTING GRIEF WITH FAITH:
SELF-CHECK QUESTIONNAIRE (December 13, 2015)

As I was sitting in my room, watching a movie, I could not help but ask myself a question. The question was "What do you desire the most, Tanisha?" What have you prayed about with unbelief? What desires have you endlessly given to God that you have not totally surrendered and given to Him?

Oftentimes, we know exactly what we want from God but aren't willing to believe. It is our way of thinking that limits our access for God to fulfill our desire. I have struggled with my thoughts for way too long to be in bondage any longer. Today (December 13, 2015) was the day that I totally took a stand and recognized the enemy for what he does.

I have learned that our very own thoughts are the most dangerous weapons in defeating grief. Willpower is derived from our thoughts. Thoughts cause us to bring actions into light. Words of light can come to you from any source. I even received enlightenment from a movie.

A movie I watched about a young blond woman opened my eyes from a spiritual perspective. The main character had many obstacles and even let her own emotions control her. However, when she made up her mind that nothing would stop her from achieving her goals, she achieved them. Of course, she had people who didn't respect her because of her personality and who she was as a person. But once she made up her mind, nothing stopped her. I loved how she would say, "I am going to show you" and "I am going to do this my way." Those statements alone reassured me that anything is possible, if we believe and have faith.
You might find it strange to have a paragraph about a movie in a section devoted to faith. That just means you need to open your mind a little wider.

The funny thing about faith is that we do not see it. We just have to know with everything in us that everything will work out. We also have to know that God is in everything we see, do, or touch. I look at faith in God as if we are blindfolded, not knowing where He will take us but trusting that He knows what we can't see.
Every desire in your heart, every word that you believe that is true, noble and righteous, give it to God. He is far able to do more than we can think and see. He is everything that we need and supplies every need or desire. I have a few questions that require a self-check that only you can do for yourself.

They are:
Are you walking in faith or fear?
Are you allowing negative thinking to lure you away from walking in your purpose?
Are you truly living what you speak (i.e., affirmations and/or Bible scriptures)?
Are you trusting God?

Tanisha A. Hall

Are you obedient (i.e., God's word and the plans that He has called you to do)?

The great thing about self-checks is that they give you the opportunity to grow and make corrections. Whatever you desire, believe and rest (see Mark 11:24 and Matthew 21:22).

Tanisha A. Hall

WHAT I'VE LEARNED AS A YOUNG WIDOW
How I want my experience from grief-based hurt to help others.

MY LESSONS FROM GRIEF

Adversity defines who we really are. Disappointment builds character. Determination brings victory. That is my aim and goal. I refuse not to have motivation. I refuse to walk in fear, doubt, and disbelief. God's word is true and will never return void. Out of all the situations I have been through, I can humbly say that losing my husband has been the most challenging. Not just because of the hurt, but because it was unexpected. I never thought in 2014 that I would have to plan a funeral, pick a plaque, and say my last goodbyes: "until we meet again." He was so content with death, I really thought he knew he would not be here long. Or maybe, it was the field that he worked in? Nevertheless, this change in my story has brought about so many obstacles and limitations. It's amazing that when we are not faced with any disappointment, we can encourage one another. However, when we have zero hope, zero strength, we forget the words we once spoke. I too have fallen into that category, in which I can barely see my way through life's disappointment.

One self-defining moment for me was when the doctors came and said that there was no hope. I refused to believe that, I was so focused on seeing him again and working through whatever needed to be done. I knew that the outcome of survival was very low. Somehow, I still didn't want to give up hope. No matter how my life has changed, I know there is a fire inside of me. A fire to live and fulfill my purpose.

Through the pain, I find strength to write about my feeling. I now live for hope. Hope for another day; hope to know that someone may be going through what I have been through. Hope that I can encourage others. Don't give up; don't lose faith during your dark season. It's only temporary. Weeping may endure for a night, but joy comes in the morning. I don't understand it, you may not either, but talk to yourself; encourage yourself in your times of darkness. Know that it's temporary. Think about the moments you felt low. Did it last forever? No! You are going to get through it. Find courage and hope by speaking to yourself daily and telling yourself who you are.

Lift up your head. You're a beautiful flower, no matter what comes your way. You will not give up! You will not lose hope! I believe in you!

I have three years of experience, living a life I never planned to have. No one has been able to advise or help me through the grief that racked me as a young widow, because I haven't met anyone else who has walked in my shoes at my age. There are things I've learned I want to share, but I also know there are things that I am still learning.

Grieving for my husband changed everything about my life. However, it would not be right to keep the information I learned in the process to myself.

We all see life through individual lenses, but that also means we can have clearer vision when we combine what we see. Please accept the following facts as information I wish someone had shared with me the day I lost my husband.

Accept the new reality for your life.
First, I'm still learning to live with this concept. If I could go back to life before my husband passed, I'd do it in a heartbeat. But that isn't going to happen so I have decided to embrace the new direction my life has taken. I also understand that this is a season. My husband is gone forever, but how I feel and felt will only last for a season. I will not let pain dictate my life. When I accepted my new reality, I began to see my true self, which means I learned incredible things about myself. This concept is hard to grasp, but looking at it in a positive light can brighten your life.

Don't allow the actions of others to dictate how you feel.
You are not qualified to judge another person's motivation for doing anything. If fact, you may have started filtering everyone's actions through the fog of emotional pain.

You're focused on you. Believe it or not, most of the people you meet are focused on themselves. That means they are not out do vindictive or malicious things that hurt you. It's just the opposite; they're trying to make sense of their own lives and struggles. So, if you walk into a room and people are talking about marriage, they're not having the conversation to hurt you. For more than a year, I didn't understand that because I was wallowing in misery. That meant certain words felt like daggers to my heart. That doesn't mean anyone aimed daggers at me. I just felt that way. The way to get rid of the pain is to understand what caused it.

Does it hurt? Yes. Are you upset? Very much so. What do you understand? Absolutely nothing. But, you cannot remain defeated.

Losing my husband affected my health and left me distraught for months. I spiraled into depression. It felt like the world had stopped moving for me. Nothing made any sense to me and all I could do was hurt. I'm not telling anyone to ignore the pain. I am saying, allow yourself time, but please by all means attempt to regain strength to take your mind off negative things.

You are going to feel or a wave of strong emotions. But find ways to push through and control them. My problem was living inside my own head and worrying about possibil-

Tanisha A. Hall

ities that would never happen. A solution to my problem was doing things I didn't want to do and interacting with people when all I wanted to do was be alone. Therefore, if your best friend wants to hang out, go!!!! He or she is not trying to make you forget about your loved one because I believe that love can never end. The important thing for you to do is not overreact over the small stuff. As best you can, take a step back and breathe.

Is grief an emotion?
In the dictionary, grief can be a noun or a verb. As a noun, it means keen mental suffering or distress. That's an understatement. Grief for me was an overwhelming flood of pain that almost destroyed me. I had never lost anyone so close to me before so I didn't know what on earth was going on with me. Grief is not just an emotion. It packs a physical wallop. I had feelings I couldn't express, and I lost a ton of weight. I had trouble eating and felt blue most of the time. What you need to know is that every feeling you have is real. Live through the moment because everything you are feeling is NORMAL!!! You are experiencing NORMAL SYMPTOMS of grief. That's not just my opinion. My therapist helped me understand this basic truth.

Every widow experiences loss differently. There are no blueprints.
Grieving was specifically hard for me because I was young. Emotionally, spiritually, and legally, few young couples prepare for death at the beginning of their lives together. That made it hard to find help. All the other widows I met were much older and had years of memories with their spouses. They had children. I never knew of any young widows. That fueled my anxiety as I began wondering about my life.

Anxiety threatened my health and sent me to a hospital emergency room. I wanted to know what was going on with me. But few medical experts had any answers. That's because, as I have learned, what may have happened for other people does not mean it will happen to you. Everyone feels pain and loss differently. Seek help inside yourself and from others. That's the only way to move forward and ultimately, the help you summon inside and outside yourself are the two strongest tools you will have to conquer grief.

Moment of Truth

I appreciate you so much for reading the journey that I embarked on as a young widow. There were many times that I did not feel confident to release this book. On several occasions I could no longer see the connection as to where I was being taken in life. However, I have come to realize that our life is a journey and it is up to us to embark the journey with love and happiness. Of course, there are bumps along the way that will lead us to lessons. Life is beautiful and we never see the beauty of life until we have no choice but to sit back and rest. Never give up on your dream because of a set back. Never tell yourself, what you can or cannot do because things did not turn out as planned. You have to learn how to dig deep and move forward. We may not have all of the answers and we may never understand. But, are you going to sit back and watch life pass you by or are you going to get into the game?! What is your moment of truth to live? What can you do to truly change and start living?! As always, I would love for you to send a prayer request so that I can be in agreement with you. Please send your prayer request to sowbeautifulflowers@gmail.com

My hope, is that this book has ministered to the deepest darkest moments in your life. I hope that you can use this book as a sense of encouragement to pursue whatever dreams and or ambitions that God has birthed through you. I hope, that this book allowed you to reflect on areas that you need growth, change and or healing. With that in mind, I would like to ask of you to do one thing.... #BREATHE to (Instagram, Twitter, Facebook and any social media outlet) and let others know the impact that this book has made in your life. Remember, we are all given talents and gifts for the uplifting of Gods Kingdom. It is however, up to us to allow those talents and gifts to shine. Again, thank you for taking the time to read my story.

Tanisha A. Hall

Thank you

I would like to first thank God for using me as a vessel for his kingdom. The journey was not easy however, I was able to get through it all because of him and the people he placed in my life.

Mom, Dad, Sheldon and Joey, I love you all dearly. I appreciate the conversations, hugs and kisses that you gave me. I appreciate you all for dealing with me even when I was not loveable. Lol. Mom and Dad, I love you for being my personal protector when I had no voice to speak up for myself at times. I love, love, love you! Sheldon and Joey, you truly are the best brothers that anyone could ask for.

Meyuna, my BFF, I appreciate you for staying with me for a month, literally. I thank you for always being the person I can call to pray for and with me. You are truly a best friend and sister anyone could ask for. We have come a long way from LHS to grown women! I appreciate you a bunches.

To my in-laws, I thank you for allowing me to be apart of your family. I appreciate you all for caring about me and loving me. It was not easy dealing with such a blow but we somehow managed to get through it all.

Mrs. Garnett, Ms. Grier and Mrs. Wright, thank you for reading the book and giving me recommendations. I greatly appreciate you all.

GoodWorks Christian Ministries, I appreciate you all for the love and support. To my Pastor Gary Turner and First Lady Mrs. Salemma Turner, thank you! I appreciate the calls and concerns when I was grieving and beyond that season in my life. You truly do not know how much I appreciate you.

To ALL of my family, friends and others that I have not stated by name, thank you! It was your prayers, love and support that has helped me along the way and to that I cannot thank you enough.

One final note, to whomever maybe reading this book, I challenge you to release fear and walk into all that you were created to be. Life struggles are never easy however, you have everything you need to be successful.